WAGE RESTRAINT:

A Study of Incomes Policies in Western Europe

WAGE RESTRAINT

A Study of Incomes Policies in Western Europe

by

Lloyd Ulman and Robert J. Flanagan

UNIVERSITY OF CALIFORNIA PRESS
Berkeley • Los Angeles • London • 1971

University of California Press
Berkeley and Los Angeles
University of California Press, Ltd.
London
ISBN: 70-153555
Library of Congress Catalog Card Number: 0-520-02024-3
Designed by W. H. Snyder

First printing 1971
Printed in the United States of America

To our wives
LASSIE and FRAN

CONTENTS

ACKNOWLEDGMENTS

This monograph has been written in the hope that an examination of past performance in major European countries might help policy makers develop guidelines for the improvement of future policies. Since one of our self-assigned tasks was to gain perspective on recent developments in the light of earlier experiments, and vice versa, our debt to the considerable literature on this subject is obvious. We have also attempted to consider policy developments in conjunction with quantitative evidence, especially since econometric and literary judgments on policy effectiveness have not always coincided. Where we thought it desirable and feasible to do so, we supplied bits of quantitative analysis ourselves; for work in this area we gratefully acknowledge the assistance of Mrs. Betty Heian. For much information and much more inspiration this study is greatly indebted to conversations with academic authorities, businessmen, government officials, and trade union leaders in the seven countries whose experience has formed the subject matter of this volume. Our debt to them is very great; however, in view of the obvious possibilities of misinterpretation and willfulness on the part of the authors, it had best be acknowledged without individual identification.

We are most grateful to Miss Joan J. Lewis, Senior Administrative Assistant in the Institute of Industrial

Relations of the University of California at Berkeley for devoted editorial and clerical assistance.

This study was made possible by a grant from the Council of Economic Advisers. It is in no sense an official document, however, and no one but the undersigned are responsible for the errors, omissions, and opinions in the pages which follow. But we are happy to acknowledge the kind and active interest of Paul W. McCracken, Hendrik S. Houthakker, and Herbert Stein of the Council.

LLOYD ULMAN

ROBERT J. FLANAGAN

INTRODUCTION:
The Problem and the Policies

The sixties ended and the seventies opened on a discouraging economic note: inflation was increasing—and had reached a rate of about 6 per cent—in the major industrial countries of the non-Communist world, while the growth of real output was declining. This divergence was not unprecedented; it furnished further evidence that deflationary measures are effective in reducing inflation only after they result in the reduction in employment and economic growth. Yet, while the juxtaposition of growing inflation and stagnation is not an infallible portent of doom, the great public concern which it has aroused is justified. For it reflects the persistence of a particularly poignant dilemma with which Western industrialized societies have been wrestling for nearly a generation: the incompatibility between politically acceptable levels of employment and either politically acceptable rates of price increase or equilibrium in the balance of payments. Having finally willed the discovery that unemployment is not an act of God (as suggested in the ancient phrase "hard times") but man-made, it was galling to accept that man should have to make it in cold blood in order to cope with inflation or external imbalance. Yet, if a politically tolerable level of unemployment (the level known popularly as "full employment") and a politically acceptable rate of price increase (known popularly as "relative price stability") could not be achieved simultaneously, it was necessary that they be approximated sequentially through alternation of deflationary and expansionary policies (known unpopularly as stop-go-stop).

In fact, postwar policy makers and the public at large have felt that they were always confronted with what the *Economist* called an "uneasy triangle" of domestic policy objectives—full employment, price stability, and free collective bargaining—any pair of which could be approximated by sacrificing the third. But when academic economists get into the act, they initially emphasized only the first two legs of the triangle in the form of a negative relationship between money wage increases and the unemployment rate. Given the importance of wages in total costs, it was but a short step to postulate a trade-off between the rates of price inflation and unemployment: the lower the rate of unemployment, the faster the rate of increase in money wages and prices. The wage-unemployment relationship—known as the Phillips curve after its discoverer—originated in empirical research and was presented essentially as a finding of fact. It was not adduced in support of a preexisting hypothesis, and, in fact, the empirical Phillips relation is itself consistent with virtually any theory of the process generating inflation. The academic popularity of the Phillips curve did not therefore rest on its ability to settle the protracted dispute between demand-pull and cost-push theories of inflation which predated its discovery.

Moreover, it was soon noted that the inflationary process was more complicated than the simple Phillips relation suggests. Econometric studies indicate that the unemployment rate is only one of several variables—including cost-of-living changes, the level or rate of change of profits, and the rate of change of unemployment itself—which are correlated with wage changes. Indeed, some economists began to argue on theoretical grounds that none of the trade-off relationships inferred from analysis of short-term fluctuations would prove stable in the long run. It was argued that while a "lax" monetary authority can initially reduce the unemployment rate to a very low level, the resulting inflation must generate inflationary expectations for which workers will seek compensation, with the result that either wages and prices will tend to rise even more rapidly (if the monetary authority persists in maintaining the low unemployment rate), or output and employment will fall, increasing the unemployment rate until it finally reaches some non-inflationary level. However, this theoretical challenge was in turn questioned by several econometric studies indicating that, within the range of postwar experience, wages and prices failed to increase by the full amount of expectations (as generated by prior movements of wages or prices). Thus, the trade-off between unemployment and inflation has remained plausible if theoretically ambiguous.

Belief in the existence of a stubborn trade-off relationship has implied belief in the limitations of monetary and fiscal policy alone to resolve the unemployment-inflation dilemma and, in some cases, the unemployment-currency crisis dilemma. For these dilemmas to be resolved (or at least reduced to politically tolerable proportions) it would be necessary to shift the Phillips curve downward, so that lower levels of unemployment could be reached without incurring such high rates of wage and price increase. For this task two additional types of policy instruments have been devised. One type, called incomes policy, was designed to restrain the behavior of organized labor and large-scale enterprise; the other, called active labor market (or manpower) policies, was designed to eliminate labor bottlenecks and (the other side of the coin) pockets of hard-core unemployment. To the extent that inflationary influences exerted by monopoly power and by bottlenecks both exist and, indeed, can be mutually reinforcing, these two lines of policy can be regarded as complementary to each other. Yet, as we shall see, they can also be competitors. Some advocates of the manpower approach, notably the Swedes, argue that, in eliminating bottlenecks, it can also deal most effectively with cost-push inflation. Others, notably some academics, feel that labor immobility is a much more important source of inflation than discretionary wage and price behavior. For, although the power of labor unions to raise wages and of large-scale enterprises to raise prices, presumptively increases as employment rises and capacity utilization in the economy increases, it is difficult to isolate and quantify the influence of discretionary wage and price behavior. On the other hand, the dispersion of occupational and industrial unemployment rates is plainly visible, and has invited emphasis on the role of bottlenecks. Moreover, the existence of labor market "frictions" can in principle generate a Phillips trade-off all by themselves; monopolistic behavior is not necessary to account for that phenomenon.

Nevertheless, restraint of monopolistic power has been regarded as almost a necessary condition for the solution of the unemployment-inflation problem. For the feeling has persisted that unrestrained exercise of excessive market and political power by large private organizations has contributed to this dilemma. These institutions helped society to secure an accommodation between modern industrial technology and political democracy; but they were developed in an era when the economic and political environment offered greater resistance to their inflationary proclivities. Have they outgrown their usefulness? Would greater decentralization of private decision-making resolve the dilemma? Could it be legislated? If so, could the new institutional forms avoid the excesses of the existing ones? Could they do so without subjecting contemporary society to dangerous intensification of those centrifugal tendencies by which it has been increasingly beset?

Holders of public office, now firmly saddled with the responsibility of avoiding unemployment as well as crises in the balance of payments, have not been unhappy to see others blamed for inflationary excesses. Yet, unsurprisingly, they have sought an alternative to drastic institutional surgery, as well as to publicly administered deflation. Thus far they have sought to avoid the excessive exercise of private power, not by eliminating the source of such power but by preventing its full exploitation. This has been the essence of what has come to be known as incomes policy. According to one theory of incomes policy, if the government sheds a "guiding light" on the "room" for increases in wages and other incomes, the private parties—aided by social pressure—see the light and restrain themselves accordingly. In application, incomes policy has come in many versions and has been used in many economic contexts, as this book indicates.

Incomes policies have generally included (although not always explicitly) four basic and interrelated elements. The first is the orientation of the policy with respect to the objectives which it is supposed to serve; the second is that group of prices and incomes which the policy is supposed to cover; the third is a guide, or norm, for the noninflationary development of incomes; the fourth is a mechanism through which enforcement is to be achieved.

Although incomes policy has always been intended to contribute to domestic price stability, it has frequently been designed to serve other objectives as well. It has also—and prominently—been designed to contribute to the country's balance-of-payments equilibrium, which means that the *levels* of costs and prices, and not merely their rates of change, become a target of incomes policy. It has sometimes been regarded as an aid in achieving a higher rate of economic growth, which might involve a diversion of resources into investment in plant and equipment and away from personal consumption. Finally, incomes policy has frequently been designed to raise the relative incomes of the poor and low-paid. Now it is unlikely that an incomes policy can serve all these objectives at once and with equal efficiency. Thus the observed differences among incomes policies with respect to their coverage, the nature of their guidelines, and their approach to enforcement reflect in part differences in national priorities.

Coverage might extend to product prices, salaries, and even property incomes, as well as wages. However, the tendency has been to emphasize the restraint of wages as an indirect approach to price stability, although some policies (especially in France) have tried to approach wage restraint through price control. As a practical matter, coverage has been determined by the degree of compulsion in the enforcement of the policy. Where the guidelines have been vague and enforcement has relied on sporadic executive exhortation, effective coverage has been limited.

The guides, or norms, have ranged from vague statements urging "noninflationary behavior" to outright wage and price freezes—a zero growth rate for all incomes. But the most common explicit wage norm has been based upon the growth of economy-wide productivity, on the arithmetic proposition that if both wage rates and output per man-hour increase at the same rate, labor costs per unit of output remain steady and there are no grounds for increasing prices on this basis. As later chapters (and experience in the United States) indicate, however, the fact that productivity growth differs among industries and that price changes frequently originate from stimuli other than labor costs requires subsidiary guide rules and often makes the general productivity guide nonoperational.

The instruments of enforcement have also varied widely. During the past decade, governments have rarely acted as if they expected social pressure from a public educated in the elements of noninflationary behavior by the publication of a norm to provide sufficient restraint on the exercise of market power. So the government has often assumed part of the burden of enforcing its norms. Its enforcement techniques have included ad hoc intervention by executive exhortation and admonition—issued in public broadcast or in private communication—the establishment of special agencies for review, before or after the fact, of wage or price actions, and blanket proscriptive regulations backed by the force of law. The extent of government intervention and the choice of enforcement devices have depended in part on the scope of coverage and the degree of detail into which the policy guidelines have gone. Thus, when changes in wage structure (as well as in the general level of wages) have been objects of the incomes policy, administrative review agencies have generally been established.

Two other types of policy must be included in this

discussion, although neither need be characterized by even a vague general wage norm. Yet both are designed to induce wage or price restraint; and the second is distinguished by active governmental enforcement. The first might be regarded as privately run incomes policy, where the central union federation—either unilaterally or in collaboration with its counterpart on the other side of the bargaining table—tries to subject wage determination to constraint in the public interest. The government, which obviously has a stake in the outcome, may or may not actively participate. If it does, its intervention might consist of encouraging the union federation to restrain its affiliates; or it might either encourage employers to raise their level of resistance to union demands or make it feasible for them to do so through increased official tolerance of industrial disputes.

The second policy category is either governmental intervention in specific product or labor markets (including markets in the public sector) or the threat of such intervention. Such actions would include reductions in tariffs or import quotas, accelerated release of government stockpiles, and the withdrawal of government orders. To the extent that such intervention is undertaken and is designed to reduce barriers to competition—resulting, in this case, from governmental protection or custom—it is akin to the "active labor market policies" discussed above. But to the extent that such action is merely threatened and is designed to induce changed behavior in the same market environment, it is a variant of incomes policy. That variant has come to be known as arm-twisting, to distinguish it from jaw-boning and ear-stroking. (Needless to say, the two approaches have not been regarded as mutually exclusive.) Moreover, when the government actively restrains the wages of its own employees, it is obviously pursuing a variant of incomes policy.

Thus, the norms and the instruments of incomes policy have varied widely, and the number of combinations in which they have appeared has been substantial. But none of the versions worked magic, and public disillusion was reflected in the decline or near-abandonment of incomes policies in the Netherlands, Britain, and elsewhere by the end of the last decade. Yet the policy's popularity in principle has thus far proved almost as durable as the problem which it was supposed to help solve. Such popularity might not be deserved, but it is understandable on two grounds. First, there is growing appreciation that its potential usefulness is limited, that it was originally oversold, and that it cannot be expected to bridge any inflationary gap, however wide. Second, the deflationary alternatives remain distasteful, and no one has yet come up with a new departure: to many policy makers, incomes policy is still the only game in town. Yet even its sturdiest proponents hope that in the future the policy might become more of a cure and less of a symptom. For the record does not hold out hope that a mere revival of the policy will prove more effective than the original versions.

But the record might help us to improve such anti-inflationary policies and more accurately to assess their future usefulness. It might help us to grapple with some hard but pertinent questions. Is incomes policy best suited to dealing with currency crises on an *ad hoc* basis? If so what are its limitations in that role? Is short-term effectiveness purchased at the expense of long-run effectiveness in abating domestic cost inflation? How effective has the policy been in the latter role? Has it worked best under conditions of overall excess demand or when there was excess capacity? Has it worked best by inducing self-restraint on the part of the trade unions or by inducing employers to resist union pressures more firmly? How important is a centralized structure as a precondition for the inducement of self-restraint; how successful might incomes policy be in shifting the locus of power and decision-making within the trade-union movement? Can other pressure groups and nonwage incomes be expected to follow unions down the straight and narrow path? Need they do so? Is some measure of governmental compulsion required? As an aid to persuasion, or as a replacement? Can the government set a good example as an employer? Can it accept incomes policy as a constraint in its efforts to minimize strike activity? What support must be provided by fiscal and monetary authorities and what constraints, if any, must they be prepared to accept if incomes policy is to be made more effective? In the following chapters these questions will be considered in the light of the experience of the major European countries which have experimented with incomes policy.

THE UNITED KINGDOM

THE APPARENT NEED FOR INCOMES POLICY

The prospects for success of incomes policy might *a priori* have appeared more favorable in the United Kingdom than in any of the other countries studied in this report. The performance of her economy was comparatively poor in a number of areas which apparently made the need for incomes policy correspondingly acute. Her political and social system was relatively stable, to this extent enhancing the policy's chances of succeeding. Yet there is a strong tendency to write off the latest series of experiments as a failure.

As in the other countries, the perceived need for incomes policy in the United Kingdom arose out of unsatisfactory performance of the economy, on the one hand, and either the apparent inefficiency of or reluctance to resort to alternative corrective measures, on the other. As elsewhere, difficulty with the balance of international payments was decisive; but in Britain an unsatisfactory rate of growth (by comparative standards) played a more important part, while domestic price inflation played a somewhat less important role in stimulating recourse to incomes policy. Periodic payments crises, aggravated by Britain's unfavorable reserve position, made for a slow rate of growth by depressing domestic investment and contributing to low incremental ratios of output to capital. This made for relatively low levels of productivity and high unit labor costs. The latter in turn tended to worsen the country's foreign-trade position, thereby completing this particular vicious circle. Moreover, managerial inefficiency and restrictive work practices helped to keep real wages low relative to capital costs; and these practices acted as further disincentives to investment in modern labor-saving equipment.[1] Thus Britain's low level of productivity[2] interacted with her unfavorable balance-of-payments position to retard the rate of growth.

Sluggish growth of productivity was primarily responsible for the rather large rates of increase in unit labor costs which Britain has experienced since the 1950's, for the rate of increase in hourly earnings in Britain has not been great, compared with the increases experienced by her industrial trading partners.[3] Nevertheless, the case for a policy to restrain the rise in wages, like the case for a policy to improve labor efficiency, did not rest on a simple performance comparison between Britain and her neighbors. Instead it depended on how effective a policy might be, relative to its economic and social costs, in improving the performance of wages and

[1] L. Ulman, "Collective Bargaining and Industrial Efficiency," in R. E. Caves and Associates, *Britain's Economic Prospects* (Washington, D.C.: The Brookings Institution, 1968), pp. 325–326. Also "Introduction," by Caves, *ibid.*, pp. 3–20.

[2] E. F. Denison, "Economic Growth," in Caves, *op. cit.*, pp. 231–278.

[3] E. H. Phelps Brown, "Guidelines for Growth and for Incomes in the United Kingdom: Some Possible Lessons for the United States," in G. P. Shultz and R. Z. Aliber, eds., *Guidelines, Informal Controls and the Market Place* (Chicago: University of Chicago Press, 1966), p. 148; L. Ulman, "Under Severe Restraint: British Incomes Policy," *Industrial Relations,* May 1967, at p. 214, n. 1; D. C. Smith, "Incomes Policy," in Caves, *op. cit.*, pp. 116–117.

productivity, because any progress along those lines would tend to improve the country's unsatisfactory balance-of-payments position, among other things.

An additional criterion of the efficiency of incomes policy consisted in its net effectiveness in relationship to the net effectiveness of alternative policy instruments. In Britain it was particularly true that, as David Smith wrote, "The case for an incomes policy has . . . depended on the case against the alternatives."[4] The cost of deflationary alternatives was obvious; in addition, their effectiveness was in doubt. Tax increases to put out balance-of-payments brush fires, followed by tax reductions to reduce unemployment, generated the cycle of "stop – go" which helped to retard growth and to prevent emergence from long-term disequilibrium in Britain's foreign accounts. Moreover, increases in indirect tax directly raised the cost of living and thus stimulated compensatory wage demands. And the effectiveness of the tax "regulator" was further diminished by "the independent life led by government expenditures" and also by the fact that tax changes were triggered by changes in employment which tended to lag a year behind changes in over-all demand.[5] Another alternative, monetary policy, shared most of the drawbacks of fiscal policy; in addition, the flexibility of this instrument (commonly regarded as an inherent advantage) was limited by the authorities' policy of protecting international reserves.[6]

An opposite alternative to deflation was more expansion. In theory, rapid growth was supposed to induce

[4] Smith, *op. cit.,* p. 106.
[5] Caves, *op. cit.,* pp. 6–7.
[6] J. H. Kareken, "Monetary Policy," in Caves, *op. cit.,* pp. 78–83.

investment and thus improve productivity and lower costs in the long run, while generating enough savings to be sufficiently noninflationary in the short run. But in practice, this type of experiment, conducted by a Conservative government, increased the volume of imports and precipitated a balance-of-payments crisis in 1964.

Finally, there was great reluctance by incumbent governments—notably the Labour government which assumed office in 1964—to devalue the currency, partly out of considerations related to national prestige and Britain's position as an international banker and partly because of the increased cost of living which such devaluation would initially entail. Reluctance to devalue underlay much of the official enthusiasm for incomes policy in Britain; official support for incomes policy began to wane after devaluation occurred in November 1967, although this coolness was due in part to the extra obstacles placed in the way of incomes policy by post-devaluation price increases.

THE POTENTIAL EFFECTIVENESS OF INCOMES POLICY

To the extent that a country's collective-bargaining institutions contribute to productive inefficiency and inflation, incomes policy is potentially effective: there is work for it to do. In Britain, the policy's work appeared to be cut out for it. The coverage of bargaining through employers' associations has been so broad that the substance of bargaining at the association level has largely been confined to a few issues, such as uniform changes in wages and hours. As a result, there has been much local wage drift; moreover, questions affecting plant productivity were separated from the official bargaining machinery to a greater extent than in the U.S. These features have been matched on the union side by virtual divorce of the officers and representatives of the national unions, whose bargaining activities were mainly confined to the industry or association level, from the shop stewards in the plants, whose autonomy and susceptibility to rank-and-file pressure made important segments of British industry unusually vulnerable to wildcat strikes.

One effect of this two-tier system of bargaining has been to make it difficult to secure the abandonment and resist the introduction of restrictive work practices and underutilization of capital equipment. The prevalence of craft unions, with narrowly defined occupational jurisdictions, has also contributed to the prevalence of make-work rules and opposition to technical change.[7] Another apparent effect of this system has been to push up wages. Association bargaining, which in Sweden and in the United States has sometimes operated to strengthen employer resistance to union demands, has operated in Britain to weaken employer resistance by setting a floor under the centrally negotiated portion of labor costs. (Britain has lost relatively little time in industrial disputes; nine-tenths of her stoppages have been local wildcat affairs.)

Thus it is not surprising that Britain's poor record of growth and productivity has been matched by a poor trade-off between changes in earnings and levels of unemployment, relative to other European countries (with the possible exception of Italy). In other words, it would take a relatively high level of unemployment to secure a given desired rate of wage change; deflationary fiscal and monetary policies would have to be severe because they would be relatively inefficient in reducing inflationary forces. That unionism has been an inflationary influence

[7] Ulman, *op. cit.*, in Caves, *op. cit.*, pp. 338–360.

is suggested by a study which shows that the percentage change in union membership provides a stronger statistical correlation with the rate of change of money wages than does the unemployment rate.[8] Another study reveals that, although the size of the drift component of earnings is affected by conditions of labor demand, the negotiated increases in wage rates have contributed independently to increases in earnings.[9]

Neither these nor other analyses imply that inflation in Britain has been a crude cost-push phenomenon; yet such results do support the widely held view that British collective bargaining has made a distinct contribution to the country's economic difficulties. In this respect it is understandable that incomes policy should have held interest for the authorities throughout much of the postwar period.

INCOMES POLICY BEFORE 1965

Before 1965, incomes policy was invoked on several occasions, primarily for the limited objective of meeting a balance-of-payments crisis.[10] In 1948, a Labour government recommended that a general rise in money incomes be foregone until matched by a corresponding growth in output. This policy worked on a purely voluntary basis for two and one half years until it dissolved in a wage explosion in 1950. Under a Conservative government in

[8] A. G. Hines, "Trade Unions and Wage Inflation in the United Kingdom, 1893–1961," *Review of Economic Studies,* October 1964.

[9] J. C. R. Dow, *The Management of the British Economy, 1945–1960* (Cambridge University Press, 1965), pp. 352–354.

[10] Detailed accounts of the earlier policies may be found in M. Edelman and R. Fleming, *The Politics of Wage-Price Decisions* (Urbana: University of Illinois Press, 1965); David C. Smith, *Incomes Policies,* Special Study No. 4 for the Economic Council of Canada (Ottawa: Queen's Printer, 1966); B. C. Roberts, *National Wages Policy in War and Peace* (London: George Allen and Unwin, 1958).

1956, however, the unions refused to exercise wage restraint despite the existence of serious balance-of-payments problems and despite the fact that the government's appeal extended to employers in their pricing policies.

Faced with another balance-of-payments crisis in the summer of 1961, the government requested a temporary wage freeze. The Trades Union Congress (TUC) again refused to cooperate with a Conservative government, but early in 1962 a White Paper set out a guideline for wage increases (2 to 2½ per cent) based on a trend in aggregate productivity. Later the five-man National Incomes Commission (NIC) was established; but it had such limited powers that its main function appeared to be educational. The NIC could review and report on wage proposals which were referred by both negotiating parties—a highly unlikely situation given the refusal of the TUC to cooperate. The commission could also review existing agreements at the request of the government but had no authority to change the provisions of any settlement.

POST 1965 INCOMES POLICY

Under the Labour government, which came to power in October 1964, incomes policy passed through five phases.[11]

1) A voluntary phase from May 1965 to July 1966 was based on the hope that a Labour government might be able to elicit union support. This support was pledged, although cautiously, in a tripartite *Joint State-*

[11] National Board for Prices and Incomes, *Report No. 122, Fourth General Report, July 1968 to July 1969,* Cmnd. 4130 (London: HMSO, July 1969), paras. 2–5; developments through 1966 are analyzed in L. Ulman, "Under Severe Restraint: British Incomes Policy" and in *Productivity, Prices and Incomes Policy After 1969,* Cmnd. 4237 (London: HMSO, December 1969), para. 7.

ment of Intent on Productivity, Prices and Incomes signed in December 1964. In 1965 the government established an administrative body, the National Board for Prices and Incomes (NBPI), to review settlements or proposals referred to it by the government; and it issued a general guideline for wage increases of 3 to 3½ per cent, with permissible exceptions and price guidelines similar to those found in the *Economic Report of the President* in 1962 and hereinafter referred to as *U.S. Guideposts*. Later in the year, the TUC attempted to forestall a compulsory requirement that the government be notified in advance of wage settlements by setting up its own procedure for internal review of wage demands by its affiliates. This was hopefully regarded as a significant cession of authority to the central federation by its autonomous affiliates. Despite these efforts, however, the rate of change of negotiated rates, hourly earnings, and retail prices continued to accelerate (rising at annual rates of 7.4, 7.6, and 5.1 per cent, respectively).

2) A statutory freeze (or "standstill") on wages and prices was in effect from July 1966 to June 1967, in response to a currency crisis. During the latter half of this period, known as a period of "severe restraint," a few minor exceptions to the freeze were allowed. In addition, the Prices and Incomes Board was placed on a statutory basis. After the freeze had been lifted, the government was to be notified at least a month in advance of any prospective increase in wages or prices, which it could at its discretion refer to the board. Agreements so referred would be subject to a "standstill" of up to three months pending a board report. (The board was to be guided by the criteria provided in the government White Paper of April 1965, referred to in the previous section.) In the periods of freeze and "severe restraint,"

hourly wage rates rose by only 2.8 per cent; hourly earnings, by 1.7 per cent; retail prices, by 2.5 per cent.

3) A relaxation or period of "moderation" from July 1967 to March 1968 was a sort of hybrid and modification of (1) and (2). Wage and price increases in excess of the norm were allowed as "exceptions" under the criteria which had prevailed during the voluntary phase. However, the norm itself continued to be zero (instead of the earlier 3 to 3½ per cent); and the government was now given statutory power to delay proposed increases in pay or prices up to seven months (including advance notice) if they were referred to the National Board for Prices and Incomes. But hourly wage rates rose by 9.2 per cent, and earnings by 8.8 per cent; although retail prices rose only 2.8 per cent.

4) A post-devaluation phase, from April to July 1968, continued the "nil norm" but allowed increases up to a ceiling of 3½ per cent when justified by labor shortages in essential situations or by pay levels which were either "too low to maintain a reasonable standard of living" or "seriously out of line with the level of remuneration for similar work" —three of the existing criteria for "exceptions." Provision was made for increases above the 3½ per cent ceiling only in cases of so-called "productivity bargaining"—where the employees concerned, "for example by accepting more exacting work or a major change in working practices, make a direct contribution towards increasing productivity in the particular firm or industry," or by accepting major revisions of internal wage and salary structures. The White Paper[12] ushering in this phase of policy also emphasized the desirability of price cuts when called for under the

[12] *Productivity, Prices and Incomes Policy in 1968 and 1969*, Cmnd. 3590 (London: HMSO, April 1968).

price criteria (i.e., where sectoral productivity is increasing faster than the appropriate rate of increase in wages and salaries; where nonlabor unit costs – materials and capital – are falling; where "profits are based on excessive market power"). This stage was extended until the end of 1969, with new statutory authority empowering the government to delay price or wage increases up to twelve months instead of only seven. For the period of April to December, 1968, hourly wage rates rose 4.5 per cent; earnings, 7.9 per cent; and retail prices, 5.5 per cent. Between January and October 1969, the increases in these categories were, respectively, 4.3, 6.6, and 5.1 per cent.

5) The statutory authority for this policy, the Prices and Incomes Act of 1968, expired at the end of 1969, and in the light of trade-union opposition as well as the approach of a general election, there was some doubt that the government would continue to promulgate any explicit guidelines. However, increases in wage rates jumped sharply in September and October, averaging 6 per cent and 8½ per cent, respectively. In December, the government issued a new White Paper which stated that most settlements should be in the range of 2½ to 4½ per cent, given a projected 3 per cent increase in output per employee.[13] In sectors where drift is substantial, negotiated wage increases should be set so that the total increase in earnings falls within the range. The White Paper stated that settlements within this range, as well as allowable exceptions, should not require price increases.

The new policy statement emphasized that all parties

[13] *Productivity, Prices and Incomes Policy After 1969,* para. 36. The pay and price increases for the subperiods referred to in the text above are taken from paras. 7 and 9.

were not to be guaranteed the $4\frac{1}{2}$ per cent ceiling, and that in practice the point within the $2\frac{1}{2}$ to $4\frac{1}{2}$ per cent range for any individual settlement would depend upon the existence of one or more conditions. These conditions, which on occasion might also justify increases above the ceiling, are: productivity agreements, reorganization of pay structures, differentially favorable treatment for low-paid workers, equal pay for women, and labor shortages. At the same time, the White Paper warned that, in the past, increases granted under such exceptional circumstances had been frequently nullified by the granting of unwarranted compensatory increases to other, relatively high-paid groups, whereby unsatisfactory wage structures were restored and the general level of wages raised.

Thus the government acknowledged past inadequacies of incomes policy, although it also claimed some measure of success. (Evidence on the policy's effectiveness will be reviewed in the following section.) Yet the two principal modifications proposed in the White Paper did not reflect an underlying determination to strengthen the policy. The first was to eliminate the National Board for Prices and Incomes and to combine its functions with those of the Monopolies Commission in a new agency to be called the Commission for Industry and Manpower. The reason given for this merger was that the increasing tendency of the Prices and Incomes Board to pass judgment on the efficiency of firms and industries in using their manpower or capital resources overlapped the work of the Monopolies Commission; in fact, there was some apparent conflict in philosophy between the two bodies. But whether this proposed change would strengthen the administration of incomes policy was extremely doubtful, since the quality and quantity of the board's decisions and the independence and zeal of its chairman (Aubrey Jones) had marked the Prices and Incomes Board as by far the most efficient element in the policy's administration.

The second administrative modification proposed in the White Paper was the extension of those provisions of the Prices and Incomes Act of 1966 (Part II) which required advance notification to the government of proposed wage and price increases and which enabled the government to delay the board up to three months. This in fact was enacted by Parliament. Since the notification requirements and the delaying powers under the 1967 and 1968 acts were to expire at the end of 1969, the reactivation of the 1966 provisions signified an intention to retain this limited sanction. On the other hand, the direct effect of the government's action was to reduce the maximum period of delay from twelve months to three. Indeed, the legislation creating the new Commission for Industry and Manpower proposed the elimination of all delaying power, although it did require advance warning.

What then, did the government really have in mind for "Productivity, Prices and Incomes Policy After 1969"? The least charitable interpretation is that the government, bowing to pressure from the trade unions but unable to jettison a policy on which it had relied heavily for a long time and which had independently attracted considerable public support, sought to preserve only enough of the fabric of incomes policy to cover its political nakedness. The most charitable interpretation is that the government wanted not to bury the policy but to put it in deep freeze—to preserve a commitment in principle and to keep some machinery in existence against a time when its prospect for success would be sufficiently improved to permit its reactivation. (This was the strategy followed by the Dutch during the wage explosion of 1963–1964.) Presumably that occasion would present itself after the next general election—and soon after, at that: for wages were rising at an annual rate in excess of 7 per cent at the beginning of this period of hibernation.

The policy's most recent decline appears to have been associated with three events of symbolic as well as intrinsic causal importance. These were: (1) the devaluation of 1967; (2) elections in two of the country's largest unions, as a result of which left-wing leaders obtained control of the national executives; and (3) replacement of the Department of Economic Affairs by the Department of Employment and Productivity as the governmental sponsor of the National Board for Prices and Incomes. These three events reflect, respectively, economic, institutional, and administrative developments.

THE POLICY'S ACTUAL EFFECTIVENESS AND THE DEVALUATION OF 1967

The ambivalence of official and private attitudes toward incomes policy may reflect professional uncertainty regarding the effectiveness of the instrument. The statistical evidence in Britain (as elsewhere), although suggestive, is ambiguous and sometimes conflicting. One conclusion, derived from the work of both David Smith and the National Board for Prices and Incomes, is that during periods when incomes policy was in effect the annual rate of increase of weekly wage rates was significantly lower—by 1 to over 2 percentage points—than the prevailing levels of unemployment and rates of change of consumer prices would have led one to predict. However, even this conclusion has been challenged by two British economists in a recent empirical study.[14] For the 1948–1968 period, Lipsey and Parkin

[14] R. G. Lipsey and J. M. Parkin, "Incomes Policy: A Reappraisal," *Economica,* May 1970, pp. 115–138.

estimated a model in which changes in weekly wage rates were explained by the unemployment rate, the rate of change of consumer prices, and the rate of change of union membership (which may be a proxy for union aggressiveness in wage bargaining). In this model, the addition of a dummy variable for periods of incomes policy improved the wage equation and indicated that wage changes were six-tenths of a percentage point lower during periods of incomes policy. Moreover, a comparison of actual wage increases during policy periods with increases predicted from equations estimated from data for periods of no policy indicated wage restraint during periods of Labour—but not Conservative—government incomes policy. However this was largely the result of restraint during the 1948–1950 Cripps policy. At best, one can infer wage restraint in the more recent period only for 1964–1966 from the prediction errors presented by Lipsey and Parkin.[15]

These authors also argue that the effect of incomes policy on the Phillips relation is *not* independent of the unemployment rate. Their empirical work, admittedly subject to a large margin of error, suggests that the specification of a wage norm induces wage restraint at unemployment rates below 1.8 per cent (British definitions) but higher than normal increases at unemployment rates above 1.8 per cent. Thus a formal incomes policy with a published wage norm could act perversely at higher levels of unemployment. Given the norm, some unionized groups might hold out for larger wage increases than they would otherwise accept under slack economic conditions.

If there is some evidence of at least occasional restraint in the advance of weekly wage rates during policy

[15] *Ibid.*, pp. 129–131.

periods, no similar effect is indicated in the behavior of hourly rates (which reflect reductions in normal weekly hours of work as well as increases in the weekly rate), or hourly earnings (which include wage drift that can be generated by informal activity of unions and employers). Smith found that, although the rate of increase in weekly rates was significantly below the predicted rate in 1965–1966, the rise in hourly rates was not, and, indeed, the rate of increase in hourly earnings was greater than expected. Smith suggested that "the policy, in focusing on wage increases in major wage negotiations [might have] induced a greater rise in other forms of economic returns, such as a shortening of normal hours at this time and a rise in wage drift."[16]

The conclusions of Lipsey and Parkin may also result from the use of weekly wage rates rather than an hourly compensation measure inclusive of drift. It is possible, for example, that an incomes policy could break the relation between changes in weekly rates and the unemployment rate (as Lipsey and Parkin argue) without breaking the relation between total hourly wage costs and the unemployment rate. However, this possibility would depend upon a fairly strong relation between the rate of change of wage drift and the unemployment rate. The evidence is mixed on this point. A study by the U.N. Economic Commission for Europe found that "in . . . the United Kingdom . . . a relationship between drift and unemployment appears . . . over much of the period—but it is a relationship which is unstable and occasionally broken."[17] But a more recent study by Gillion found that the drift of earnings above wage rates is partly explained by the rate of change in

[16] Smith, *op. cit.,* in Caves, *op. cit.,* pp. 133–134.

[17] Economic Commission for Europe, *Incomes in Post-War Europe* (Geneva, 1967), Chapter 3, p. 22.

unemployment and not by the level of unemployment or by price changes; whereas the latter two variables are related to changes in rates.[18] These results differ from the finding by Dow referred to above (footnote 9), but it is consistent with an analysis by Flanagan. This model explains changes in earnings in terms of all three variables—the level and rate of change of unemployment and the rate of change of retail prices.[19] The level of unemployment is frequently regarded as a proxy for the level of excess demand in the economy, whereas its rate of change is sometimes taken as a proxy for expectations of future business conditions. Thus interpreted, both variables would help to determine the level of union bargaining power at a given point in time.

Phelps Brown[20] and others have emphasized that industrywide bargaining has exerted an inflationary influence on wage rates in Britain—since it removes the fear of being undercut on labor costs by one's competitor. By the same token, industrywide bargaining should also serve as an effective vehicle for restraint through incomes policy, since it should provide assurance to a member firm that it need not fear being outbid for labor by its competitors in the employers' association. But although

[18] C. Gillion, "Wage Rates, Earnings, and Wage Drift," *National Institute Economic Review,* November 1968, p. 61.

[19] R. J. Flanagan, "An International Study of Phillips Curves," unpublished Ph.D. dissertation, Berkeley, University of California, 1970, p. 88. Quarterly data for 1951-I to 1968-IV yield the equation:

$$\dot{E} = 3.01 + \underset{(3.79)}{12.59}\, U^{-2} - \underset{(1.27)}{3.23}\, \dot{U} + \underset{(.08)}{.48}\, \dot{P} \qquad R^2 = .54$$

in which $\dot{E}$ is the rate of change of earnings, U is the aggregate unemployment rate, $\dot{P}$ is the rate of change of retail prices, and the standard errors are in parentheses.

[20] E. H. Phelps Brown, *The Growth of British Industrial Relations* (London: Macmillan, 1959), pp. 124–125, 161–163, 267–270, 358–367.

industrywide bargaining can thus minimize the fear of competitive disadvantage, it need not dull the offensive spirit. An employer might still find it tempting or feasible to grant something extra at the plant level to the extent that he believes that prospective conditions of demand for his product will enable him to absorb the extra cost in higher prices without (proportionate) loss of sales. At the same time, union bargaining power, restrained by incomes policy at the upper tier, might be deflected downwards to the level of the shop stewards, where invidious intraindustry comparisons are always being made. Thus, while incomes policy might be effective in reducing the influence of excess demand on union bargaining power and wage rates at the industry level, it might generate increased pressure on earnings at the grass roots, where its ability to do so would depend on employer assessments of future conditions of product demand and the cost of resisting demands by local groups.

The Prices and Incomes Board, in addition to crediting incomes policy with restraining wage increases, pointed with cautious pride to an unusually big increase in productivity relative to unemployment and unfilled vacancies, which occurred after the 1966–1967 squeeze. As a result, while the annual rate of increase in hourly earnings jumped to almost 9 per cent during the period of "moderation" (July 1967 to March 1968), unit wage and salary costs rose by only 4.3 per cent. And during the remainder of 1968, when earnings rose at an annual rate of 8 per cent, payroll costs per unit of output rose by only 1.9 per cent. In contrast, a slightly lower rate of increase in hourly earnings in the prefreeze period (April 1965 to June 1966) was associated with a rise of 7 per cent in wage and salary costs per unit of output.

According to the Board:

It is possible that one factor to have contributed to this rise in productivity has been the emphasis placed on the productivity criterion in the current productivity, prices and incomes policy; the productivity component has already been there, but it has been brought much more to the forefront than in previous phases of incomes policy—for example, in 1948–50 and 1961–62. What may have happened is that the "squeeze" of 1966 brought about a "shake-out" of labour and the emphasis on productivity later contributed to stricter manning standards.[21]

To the extent that incomes policy has been effective in raising the growth rate of productivity (or in restraining wage increases) it should also have been a restraining influence on prices. However, there is virtually no evidence pointing in this direction; indeed in one study a statistically significant dummy variable implied that the rate of price increase was actually 1-1½ per cent greater during periods of incomes policy than one would have predicted on the basis of changes in wages and import prices.[22]

Smith claimed evidence of two apparent exceptions during the voluntary freeze of 1948–1950 and especially in the 1966–1967 period, when (after allowance for the introduction of the selective employment tax in the latter period) retail price increases were below predicted values.[23] During these periods the behavior of wages was also noticeably restrained. However, Lipsey and Parkin find retail price increases were generally

[21] National Board for Prices and Incomes, *Report No. 122,* para. 19.

[22] R. G. Bodkin, E. P. Bond, G. L. Reuber, and T. R. Robinson, *Price Stability and High Employment,* Special Study No. 5, prepared for The Economic Council of Canada (Ottawa: Queen's Printer, 1967), pp. 238–239.

[23] Smith, *op. cit.,* in Caves, *op. cit.,* pp. 134–135, 142.

greater than predicted during the 1948–1950 period and were most restrained during the 1956 policy period (under a Conservative government).[24]

The 1966–1967 experience suggests that the effectiveness of incomes policy was greater when the policy was backed by strong governmental compulsion. However, the board's own preliminary study found no apparent difference in effectiveness between the years when the policy was "essentially voluntary" (1948–1950 and 1965) and the "years of tight control" (1961–1962 and 1966–1967). The relevant coefficients in this study are not statistically significant;[25] but the inference drawn from this econometric analysis squares with the widely held opinion that the success of the 1966–1967 freeze was due to voluntary acceptance and self-restraint, with governmental sanctions kept in reserve to deal only with the "rogue elephant."

The experiences of 1948–1950 and of 1966–1967 suggest two other attributes which might be characteristic of an effective incomes policy. The first is the "nil norm." The absolute freeze seems to be more operational than wage and price guideposts based on past or anticipated movements in over-all and sectoral productivity—which seldom if ever yield to generally accepted measurement—or on "exceptions" which invite abuse.

The second attribute is that the effectiveness of an effective policy is likely to be only temporary; indeed the experience of July 1967 to March 1968 shows how a period of effective restraint can be succeeded by a wage

[24] Lipsey and Parkin, *op. cit.*, pp. 130–131. Their plot of prediction errors indicates that 1966 price increases were also considerably less than predicted.

[25] National Board for Prices and Incomes, *Report No. 77, Third General Report, August 1967 to July 1968,* Cmnd. 3715 (London: HMSO, July 1968), Appendix A, para. 9.

"explosion": earnings rose from an annual rate of 1.7 per cent to 8.8 per cent while the rate of increase in retail prices remained virtually unchanged at 2.8 per cent. Econometric studies have shown the same phenomenon of temporary effectiveness, since dummy variables which tested for a once-and-for-all improvement in the wage change-unemployment tradeoff relationship during periods when incomes policies were officially in effect proved to be more significant explanatory variables than did dummies which allowed for a gradual increase in effectiveness.[26] This result is discouraging to proponents of the original theory underlying incomes policy: that it would be increasingly effective in inducing institutional self-restraint through education and guidance over a range of economic conditions subject to discretionary wage-setting. From this viewpoint any short-term effectiveness achieved by a crash program, characterized by an unqualified zero norm and by governmental enforcement, is purchased at the expense of long-term educational effectiveness. (Dieticians tend to hold a similar view.) The White Paper of 1969 sadly observed:

> The lesson of the past few years is that the use of a productivity, prices and incomes policy for short-term purposes can only have a short-term effect. The long-term role of the policy is essentially an educational one: designed to bring home the fact that continuing steady expansion of the economy depends on our striking the right balance between an immediate increase in consumption and the long-term needs of economic development. . . . In moving towards the long-term development of the policy the Government will be placing more reliance on its educational role, but the need to learn the lessons of economic choice *is as urgent as ever it was.*[27]

[26] Bodkin, *op. cit.*, p. 236; Smith, *op. cit.*, in Caves, *op. cit.*, p. 134.
[27] Cmnd. 4237, *op. cit.*, para. 10. Our italics.

But the policy had to be diverted to short-run purposes because it had failed as a gentle educational corrective to obviate the need to resort to harsh short-run expedients. Thus incomes policy under the Wilson government was designed to forestall currency crises and thus make devaluation unnecessary. But, given the failure of the initial voluntary phase when earnings rose 7½ per cent, the policy obviously did nothing to prevent a currency crisis in the summer of 1966. The latter forced a wage freeze; and although the freeze was successful, its effects were not sufficiently large or prolonged to prevent a tardy devaluation in November 1967. Devaluation, in turn, complicated life for the less stringent incomes policy of the time, since it tended—and indeed was intended—to restrain domestic consumption by inducing a rise in the cost of imports. This induced the Prices and Incomes Board to demonstrate good faith to the unions by emphasizing price restraint, although the main thrust of British incomes policy had traditionally been directed at wages and although this approach would have been more consistent with post-devaluation requirements. Thus an originally overburdened incomes policy was further strained by a devaluation by helping to delay its predicted impact on the balance of payments.

DETERIORATION OF TRADE UNION SUPPORT

The failure of incomes policy to teach "the lessons of economic choice" is clearly reflected in trade-union reaction. Union reaction moved from an initial position of official acceptance, often combined with *de facto* disregard, to genuine cooperation during the "standstill" period in the latter half of 1966, and thence to increasing disaffection and, finally, virtually open disregard. It had been expected on the basis of postwar experience that the Trades Union Congress would not deny to a Labour government the cooperation which it had withheld from Conservative governments. It is probably true that the measure of support which the TUC granted the Wilson government was in fact greater than the support which it would have granted to a Tory regime under similar circumstances. Nevertheless, the British experience seems to indicate that the existence of a Socialist government by no means constitutes a sufficient condition for effective union support of incomes policy.

One of the principal arguments by George Woodcock (then general secretary of the Trades Union Congress) was that if the TUC and its affiliates supported the incomes policy of "their" government, they would, in return, earn the right to be consulted in all areas of high public policy, foreign and domestic—and especially in the formulation and execution of a national economic plan. Woodcock later complained that neither he nor his colleagues on the TUC's General Council were being systematically consulted in this manner, but, even if they had been, it is extremely doubtful whether the heads of the national unions—not to mention the membership—would have favored a sacrifice of collective bargaining in the interests of the political wing of the trade union movement, that is, away from the affiliated national unions and in favor of the traditionally weak central federation.

As noted above, the TUC did set up an Incomes Policy Committee in 1965 to which all wage demands were to be referred as the first step in the government's voluntary "early warning system." This action was taken, however, in an effort to head off the threat of compulsory legislation made by the government after the wage norm of 1965 had been substantially breached. And although the "vetting" committee handled hundreds of claims, the claims were not particularly subdued, and the committee never asked the Minister of Labour to refer a single case to the Prices and Incomes Board.

After the freeze the TUC revised its wage-vetting machinery, this time in order to head off a government suggestion that a tripartite screening system be established. In addition, the TUC decided to operate its own incomes policy by publishing its own economic reports and forecasts, complete with norms for wage increases. In 1967 and 1969, these reports concluded that wage incomes could safely be allowed to rise by 5 and 6 per cent respectively, based on growth projections approximately twice as great as those put forth by the government. Yet the 1969 Conference of Executives was unenthusiastic in its support of even this home-grown policy; indeed, the big left-wing-led Amalgamated Union of Engineering and Foundry Workers had earlier withdrawn its cooperation from the TUC committee. Meanwhile, the TUC itself had shifted its resources and energies to the unfamiliar task of improving collective-bargaining machinery and damping industrial conflict—this time as part of a temporarily successful attempt to head off government-sponsored industrial relations legislation.

In linking incomes policy to economic planning and seeking to sell it as a necessary condition of growth in real incomes, the British appreciated the need to sugar-coat the pill with special allowances for productivity bargaining and for low-paid workers. The first was an appeal to the baser instincts of the well-organized trade unionists; the second, to their altruism. Productivity bargaining might well prove to be the most enduring accomplishment of British incomes policies in the 1960's. Nevertheless, it is subject to obvious abuse; and much of its success is conditioned on the prior effectiveness of a policy of wage restraint. In the absence of an effective guidepost, it is not really necessary to "earn" an exception, unless management feels sufficiently constrained to drive a tough bargain. On the other hand, if the parties do wish to conclude genuine productivity bargains, they do not need an incomes policy to do it (note the negotiation of the so-called mechanization and modernization agreement in the U.S. West Coast longshore industry).

For a redistribution of income in favor of·low-paid workers, however, a policy of wage restraint by the more affluent is necessary to narrow occupational and industrial wage structures. Both the Prime Minister and the General Secretary of the TUC leaned heavily on this redistributional feature of the policy in an appeal to the Socialist conscience of the British unions. The TUC in turn sought support for an accretion of its own power over the affiliated national unions, in operating its wage-vetting program in this same vein of egalitarianism and altruism. In 1967, one of their officials said, "Now we'll see whether or not we have a labor movement." Today, he presumably is still looking.

As in Sweden and the Netherlands—where the power or influence of the central federations is much greater—the higher-paid workers, and especially the salaried white-collar groups, have not been content to see their relative pay standing diminished. Unions in low-wage industries favored incomes policies; prominent in opposition were leaders of white-collar groups (e.g., draftsmen, technicians, low-level supervisors) whose left-wing political arguments (against military spending, and so on) complemented the maximizing proclivities of their constituents. More highly paid blue-collar groups did support the low-wage exceptions in the policy, but were accused by the government of using the claims of their low-wage colleagues to justify their own demands (in the name of "equity" or "traditional differentials").[28] David Smith found no evidence that the dispersion of wage increases was reduced in 1961–1962 and 1966–1967, the years when incomes policy was most vigorously pursued.[29]

Attempts to eliminate sex differentials in pay tended to encounter the same obstacle. Although the Labour government decided that minimum-wage legislation would not be an effective device for increasing the relative earnings of low-paid workers,[30] it decided to legislate on equal pay for women. But it warned:

> By definition moves towards equal pay for women cannot be used as arguments for increasing men's rates of pay; nor should they be used as arguments for increases in the pay of those women who already enjoy equality in rates. . . . Like all such moves it involves changes in traditional pay differentials.[31]

In the background was a long and bitter strike at the Ford Motor Company for elimination of the sex differential. The company had originally offered this in negotiations—it had comparatively few women employees—but the union side refused it as unacceptable to the men.

The TUC acknowledges its own inability to administer a redistribution of income in favor of low-paid unionists, but it remains convinced that such redistribution is a necessary condition for union acceptance of

[28] *Ibid.*, para. 68.

[29] Smith, *op. cit.*, in Caves, *op. cit.*, pp. 135–136.

[30] The White Paper of 1969 rejected the proposal of a statutory minimum wage on the grounds that a large majority of the low-paid workers are in industries where average pay is relatively high; this presents the possibility that the other workers might take the national minimum "as a new base on which to rebuild their existing differentials," in which case "the cost of living would rise sharply; and the low paid would in the end be no better off" (para. 63).

[31] *Ibid.*, para. 79.

incomes policy. However, it now insists that incomes policy be regarded as including fiscal policy appropriate to redistributive objectives and minimum-wage legislation, as well as wage-price restraint.

It is also acknowledged that the membership, although less willing than the leadership to accept restraint in furtherance of economic growth, social justice and a Labour government, may be more willing to accept higher levels of unemployment than they were in the past. When in 1966 Wilson cautiously announced that unemployment rates of as high as 2 per cent might henceforth be acceptable, union spokesmen protested volubly, as did a fair number of journalists. In 1968 and 1969, however, unemployment was steady at close to 2½ per cent (4–5 per cent by U.S. definitions); and, although this was originally regarded as a temporary post-devaluation expedient, its persistence does not appear to have generated significant unrest. When groups of unionists in depressed areas like Wales were asked to specify public problems of greatest concern to them, unemployment did not rank particularly high on the lists. This doubtless reflects the ameliorating effects of recently enacted programs of earnings-related supplements to unemployment benefits (1965) and redundancy payments (1966); if so, it could mean that a somewhat greater public tolerance of unemployment has been generated as one by-product of these transfer payments.

These considerations suggest to us an expected-loss theory of membership rejection of incomes policy. Assuming that the policy is successful in meeting the educational objective of making unionists appreciate the Phillips trade-off and that the alternative to wage restraint is deflation, it by no means follows that they will prefer the former. Only a very small minority of wage earners have reason to fear loss of their own jobs under modern deflationary conditions; the great majority would have to forego some wage increases under an effective incomes policy.

In one structural respect the British system of trade unionism and collective bargaining appears to be more amenable to acceptance of incomes policy than the American system. As noted above, the officers of British national unions spend relatively little time on bargaining business, by American standards, and a good deal of time on TUC, Labour party, and governmental affairs. As a result, most national-union officials were more amenable to influence from the TUC and the Labour government in carrying out incomes policy than their American counterparts would be if the president of the AFL-CIO decided to try to cooperate actively with the government in this area. But if the central federation has—or has had—more influence over the affiliated national unions under the British system, the latter have in general much less control over plant-level units and bargaining than national unions in the United States. This is especially true of unions in industrial jurisdictions characterized by significant industry-wide competition or significant concentration in product markets. This helps to account for the problem of drift, which, as noted above, is partly the product of bargaining by highly autonomous shop stewards. The bargaining and the political power of these stewards is related to their ability to call—and to the willingness of uninvolved groups to honor—wildcat strikes. Given the generally lower level of their economic sophistication, their proximity and susceptibility to rank-and-file pressure, and, in a good number of cases, their left-wing proclivities, the British shop stewards have proved formidable opponents of incomes policy.

Moreover, their strength became reflected more

directly at the top levels of the national union and the TUC itself. As a result of elections in the late sixties (participated in as usual by about 5 per cent of the membership) the top executive positions in two of the largest unions—the Amalgamated Engineering Federation (AEF) and the Transport and General Workers' Union—passed into left-wing hands. The two new chief executives were elected with shop steward support. In 1969, in reaction to reductions in work force announced as a result of the merger between British G. E. and English Electric, a group of shop stewards proposed that employees seize some of the plants and proceed to run them as cooperative enterprises—a form of do-it-yourself "participation." They were decisively rebuffed by the workers—but their Institute of Worker Control had been supported by the left-wing leaders referred to above. On the other hand, in a subsequent strike at Ford Motor Company, there is some evidence that the national leadership of the AEF opposed the militant stewards when a majority of the employees favored acceptance of a company offer of an 18 per cent wage increase. Nevertheless, under their new leadership, the Engineers and the General Workers tipped the voting balance of the Congress from a rather narrow margin in support of the government—if not of incomes policy per se—to a decisive vote against any legislative policy. And it is generally agreed that the views of the new trade-union left on incomes policy does faithfully represent rank-and-file opinion.

Finally, the prospects of incomes policy were worsened by the government's ignominious attempt to introduce a very mild form of industrial-relations legislation. In fact, it was reportedly as a result of the inability of the Cabinet to agree on the future of incomes policy that the government decided to emphasize the wildcat strike problem and concentrate on trade-union reform. They tried two sales pitches on the trade unions: (a) if you don't acquiesce in the Labour party's measures, you will fare worse under the Tories; and (b) if you accept this reform package, the government will reduce the present twelve months' maximum freeze on wage increases referred to the Prices and Incomes Board to four months (as originally provided in the 1966 legislation). The unions rejected the deal, regarding any reform legislation as an entering wedge. Moreover, they felt that proposal (b) was not a genuine *quid pro quo,* that the government had been planning to reduce the maximum delay period in any event. And after the government—under threat of backbench rebellion, an open schism between the trade union and Parliamentary wings of the Labour party, and possibly even political strikes—drew the few remaining teeth from their industrial-relations proposals, the unions followed that victory with a demand that all prices and incomes legislation be dropped. (They narrowly and unenthusiastically voted continuing support of the TUC's own version of incomes policy. But by this time, the main energies of the TUC executive had been turned to setting up machinery to enable the Congress to settle jurisdictional disputes and strikes and to reform collective-bargaining procedures. They had agreed to do this when the Prime Minister dropped the proposed industrial-relations bill of 1969.)

PRICE STABILITY VERSUS INDUSTRIAL PEACE

The National Board for Prices and Incomes was established as an independent (nongovernmental) agency, but it was not given authority to undertake investigations on its own initiative; it had to depend on a designated governmental department for its references. Thus the board's effectiveness was limited by the sponsoring department's own zeal and efficiency. "In this respect," the board's Fourth General Report noted wistfully, "the Board differs from the recently established Canadian Prices and Incomes Commission, which 'will not be compelled to accept such references from the Government if other priorities exist or if it feels that a particular reference is not relevant to its primary function. The Commission will also be free to indicate its own inquiries on any matter falling within the jurisdictional field of the Federal Government.'"[32]

After April 1968, the board operated under the sponsorship of the Department of Employment and Productivity (DEP), formerly the Ministry of Labour. Before then, it had been responsible to the Department of Economic Affairs. The latter was generally entrusted with problems related to growth, productivity, and planning; and its personnel regarded incomes policy as an important adjunct to these areas. It was also a new department, however, and some senior civil servants in the Treasury and the Ministry of Labour regarded it as an interloper; it has since been reorganized out of existence.

The board was apprehensive over its 1968 transfer on two grounds. In the first place, it doubted whether price references, which had to be sponsored by other agencies (like the Board of Trade and the Ministry of Technology) would be as readily transmitted to and through DEP as they had been under the old sponsor. In the second place, transferring wage references to a Labour Department

[32] National Board for Prices and Incomes, *Report No. 122*, pp. 13–14. The charge to the Canadian Prices and Incomes Commission is quoted from *Policies for Price Stability*, Government of Canada, 1968, para. 71.

would place the most crucial area of incomes policy in the hands of those officials most directly responsible for minimizing industrial conflict and most responsive to the trade union constituency. In the 1969 General Report, the board observed that "Strikes are in any case a symptom, and too much concentration on them may lead to a distraction from the problem of cost inflation." But the government chose to give effect to the DEP's subjective trade-off between wage-price stability and industrial peace, because it decided to concentrate on industrial relations reform rather than on incomes policy.

According to one version, it was failure to reach agreement within the Cabinet on the future of incomes policy which led the Chancellor of the Exchequer to substitute reference to reform legislation for a paragraph on incomes policy in his budget message. That he could and wished to regard these two policy areas as substitutes is regarded in some quarters as reflecting the influence of the International Monetary Fund and Britain's other creditors, who allegedly have attached to their loans the condition that "you do something about the bloody unions." Either incomes policy or reform of industrial relations would serve that purpose.

In any event, the board's report made clear its feeling that in the fiscal year 1969–1970 its total number of references, and especially its price references, markedly declined.[33] This charge was generally accepted and borne with equanimity in the Department of Employment and Productivity. The DEP was accused of allowing some sour "exceptions," including some fairly empty pay-and-productivity bargains. As might be imagined, it was prone to "turn a Nelson's Eye" to excessive pay increases when nationally important strikes were threat-

[33] *Ibid.*, pp. 14–15.

ened. In the late sixties this allegedly occurred in disputes involving the draftsmen's union and the engineering industry, the Concorde aircraft project, Rolls Royce (after it had received a very large export order), the docks, railroads, and coal mines. According to some employers, some unions deliberately pressed for wage increases in areas where they knew the government couldn't stand a strike. Such policy lapses in turn induced pay claims by groups whose original settlements had been negotiated within the guidelines, on the mistaken assumption that the incomes policy would be generally enforced.[34]

CONCLUSIONS AND PROSPECTS

Incomes policy was prosecuted vigorously in the United Kingdom, under a Labour government, in the latter half of the 1960's. It was viewed hopefully as a way of raising productivity and moderating inflation, and as an alternative to currency devaluation. It owed much of its popularity to the prevailing conviction that the British collective-bargaining system caused wage inflation and retarded industrial progress, thereby contributing to the economy's unfavorable trade-off relationship between money wage changes and unemployment and to its comparatively slow growth.

The effectiveness of the policy, however, is in some doubt. It seems to have been most successful in restraining the rise in wage rates negotiated at industry-wide (or multi-industrial) levels, but this restraint was to a considerable extent offset by the drift of hourly earnings generated at the local or plant level. It played a major

[34] See, for example, the discussion of the teachers' strike in *The Economist,* January 10, 1970, p. 19.

role in stimulating recourse to pay-and-productivity agreements; and might thus have contributed to an apparent rise in trend productivity. But it does not appear to have exerted, either directly or indirectly, a restraining influence on price movements, except during the freeze period of 1966–1967. Its effectiveness in restraining wages was most evident during that period and during an earlier freeze in 1948–1950. This experience suggests that incomes policy in Britain has been most effective: (a) under a Labour government, (b) under a zero norm (or guideline) for wages, (c) when a currency crisis threatened the country, and (d) when (as in 1966–1967 but not in 1948–1950) popular support was buttressed by governmental sanctions. On the other hand, the apparent failure of the policy after 1967 suggests that none of these conditions suffices for the effectiveness of incomes policy. Finally, the policy's effectiveness appears to have been a temporary phenomenon, frequently to be followed by wage "explosions"; and effective "freezes" might have been bought at the expense of the long-run mission of modifying institutional behavior through education and persuasion. Support for the policy, although solicited in the interests of economic growth and of the working poor, was never appreciable at the level of the grass roots in the labor movement; and the resistance of shop stewards, left-wing union leaders, and white-collar groups ultimately eroded official support by the Trades Union Congress and forced the Wilson government to strike its colors.

With the election of a Conservative government in June 1970 the prospects for yet another revival of incomes policy in the United Kingdom appeared to grow even dimmer. Like the Republicans under Nixon, the

Conservatives under Heath announced their opposition to incomes policy even before they assumed office. In part their opposition was ideological; the negative *a priori* verdict of laissez-faire economics, pronounced mainly by academic economists in the United States, was put forth by a faction of the Conservative party, led by Enoch Powell, in Britain. On the other hand, employer support of incomes policy has not been inconsiderable in Britain and in the Conservative party; employers generally have been likely to differ from some academic opinion in their assessment of the inflationary potential of British unionism. Thus Conservative opposition to incomes policy was not predominantly ideological, but stemmed instead from at least two other sources.

The first of these was the emphasis placed by the Tories on securing legislative restraints on some aspects of collective bargaining and union activity. In the late 1960's the Conservative party called for the adoption of such measures as determination of bargaining units by a Commission on Industrial Relations, legal enforcement of collective contracts, and the withdrawal of legal protection from sympathetic strikes and strikes in furtherance of the closed shop and jurisdictional disputes. The main thrust of such changes, from the employers' viewpoint, is the abatement of the wildcat-strike problem, which has been widely regarded as exerting a debilitating effect on plant efficiency and the propensity to innovate. Thus many employers and others in the Conservative-party establishment consider that collective bargaining reform, by raising trend productivity, would improve the inflation-unemployment trade-off and thus further the objectives of incomes policy. Indeed, some would regard reform as a complement to incomes policy and not as a substitute, despite their criticism of the policy as administered by a Labour government. Nevertheless, industrial-relations reform and incomes policy might be regarded as competing political alternatives by a Conservative government, just as they had been by a Labour government, at least initially. An approach based on the imposition of some restrictions on union bargaining power is a horse of a different color from an approach which calls upon the unions to refrain from full utilization of their (intact) bargaining power; and it would be a neat trick to ride both of these steeds at once. The Tories gave every evidence of assigning absolute priority to the former approach.

The second decisive reason for the Conservatives' rejection of incomes policy was that it had been taken over by a Labour government and had been widely regarded as a failure. Indeed, this source of opposition supported the others mentioned above; the failure of the policy under Labour strengthened the influence of the Powellite school of thought within the Conservative party and also made out a powerful political case for industrial relations reform (in part by supporting the inference that any cost incurred in terms of diminished recourse to incomes policy would be negligible).

Indeed, the apparent evidence of the failure of post-devaluation incomes policy is dramatic. It is simply, as the following table shows, the coexistence of exceptionally high rates of both wage inflation and unemployment: According to our estimating equation (footnote 19), the increases in hourly earnings in 1968 and 1969 exceeded those estimated on the basis of prevailing levels of unemployment and of price changes.

At the same time evidence of the policy's past failure was regarded by some as making out a case for its revival. How could the new government reflate a stagnant economy which gave every evidence of diverting any incremental demand into wage and price increases

UNEMPLOYMENT, WAGE AND PRICE CHANGES IN THE UNITED KINGDOM, 1960–1969

	Average 1960-1967	1968	1969
Unemployment as per cent of labor force (G.B.)	1.8	2.4	2.4
Annual percentage rates of increase in:			
Hourly wage rates (U.K.)	5.1	7.7	5.4
Wage drift (U.K.)	1.2	−0.3	2.0
Hourly earnings (U.K.)	6.3	7.4	7.4
Labor costs per unit of output	3.2*	4.0	5.6
Retail prices	3.4*	4.7	5.4

*1962–1967

SOURCE: *Employment and Productivity Gazette,* June, 1970, pp. 526, 549, 258 and 262.

instead of increases in output, productivity, and employment? (However, the high drift at 2.4 per cent unemployment in 1969 disturbingly suggests the existence of a substantial "autonomous" component of drift—and of the consequent limitations of even a successful incomes policy, by past standards.) Any temptation to damn the inflationary torpedoes and sail full steam ahead would be successfully quashed by memories of the past Conservative government in 1964. The political case for a revival of an unsuccessful policy would be *faute de mieux,* but it could be no less persuasive for that. Of course, a much more powerful case would be provided by the advent of a crisis in the balance of payments. With the memory of 1965–1967 still painfully green, it is not to be expected that the government would overburden incomes policy by regarding it as a viable alternative to currency devaluation; but it could well decide to reinvigorate the policy in the aftermath of a devaluation.

At any rate, the existence of a balance-of-payments crisis might again serve as virtually a sufficient condition for the reinvigoration of incomes policy.

Even in the absence of serious external disequilibrium, domestic economic problems might suffice to overcome the obstacles in the way of a policy comeback. Indeed, something akin to a revival appeared during the summer of 1970 when government authorities announced their determination to resist pending claims for excessive increases on the part of such groups in the public sector as: local government manual workers (37 per cent), coal miners (25 per cent), teachers (40 per cent), railwaymen (25 per cent), busmen (25 per cent). (Such claims tend to be open-ended as to duration; in some cases they followed settlements made less than six months previously.)[35] To the extent that it seeks to impose restraint in its capacity as an employer, the present Conservative government can find some precedent in the "pay pause" of 1961 when, under the leadership of Chancellor Selwyn Lloyd, an earlier Conservative government decided to take the initiative by freezing civil-service salaries. That was done, however, in response to a balance-of-payments emergency; moreover, the private sector refused to follow the lead given by the public sector.[36] The summer of 1970 was to some extent distinguished from the summer of 1961 in that the initiative came more from the public-employee groups whose wage demands, in an accelerating inflation, were so high as to make some governmental response virtually inevitable. Nevertheless, the lesson taught by the aftermath of the Selwyn Lloyd pay pause remains relevant.

[35] *The Economist,* September 5, 1970, p. 79.

[36] David C. Smith, *Incomes Policies: Some Foreign Experiences and Their Relevance for Canada* (Ottawa: Queen's Printer, 1966), pp. 109–110.

THE NETHERLANDS

In the Netherlands, incomes policy has found its most determined and innovative supporters. Yet in retrospect it appears that much of this determination and innovation was devoted to replacing some of the original bases of the policy's early success. This tack has taken Dutch incomes policy through a succession of phases, which have been well described in the literature and which we have taken the liberty of summarizing in tabular form, with respect to only a few of their salient characteristics. The obvious and probable cost of this extreme form of compression is found in its tendency to overdramatize some distinctions and to play down important elements of continuity. But the chronology does enable us to avoid repetitious discussion of material well treated in the literature,[1] and to focus our attention on some bases of the apparent early success of Dutch incomes policy between the end of World War II and the Korean War, on their rejection by private parties, on the shortcomings of subsequent policy modifications, and on attempts begun in the late 1960's to establish new bases on which incomes policy might be revived.

[1] For some very perceptive and helpful sources, see M. Edelman and R. W. Fleming, *The Politics of Wage-Price Decisions* (Urbana: University of Illinois Press, 1965), Chapter 5; D. C. Smith, *Incomes Policies* (Ottawa: Queen's Printer, 1966), Chapter 6; and J. P. Windmuller, *Labor Relations in The Netherlands* (Ithaca: Cornell University Press, 1969), Chapters 7 and 8.

BASES OF EARLY SUCCESS

Structural characteristics.

The first important lesson taught by the Dutch is in some respects a negative one. It has frequently been asserted that the prospect for a successful incomes policy is an increasing function of the degree of centralization of a country's wage- and price-setting institutions. The Dutch experience casts no doubt on the importance of centralization thus formulated, but it does establish that extreme centralization—for example, along Swedish lines—is not a necessary condition for policy effectiveness. For Dutch labor markets have not been centrally organized in this fashion. Union organization has been neither complete nor uniform. Some 40 per cent of Dutch wage and salary workers are union members; and the degree of organization ranges from 27 per cent in clothing and textiles to 79 per cent in mining. Moreover, Dutch unionists are, in the Continental manner, organized along political and confessional lines. The largest grouping is the Socialist-affiliated Netherlands Federation of Trade Unions (NVV), whose 550,000 members constitute 14 per cent of wage and salary employment. The two confessional federations are the Catholic Workers' Movement (NKV) with about 420,000 members, and the Protestant Labor Federation (CNV) with about 240,000 members.[2] Since each federation's affiliated unions are normally organized along industrial lines, this makes for plural unionism at the level of the industry and, indeed, of the firm and plant. In addition, another 290,000 workers have joined independent,

[2]Windmuller, *op. cit.*, p. 189. However, more than a quarter of all Dutch union members are in the building, construction, and steel-and-metal fabricating industries which have frequently been leaders in postwar negotiations.

Some Salient Departures in Dutch Wage-Price Policies

Wage Policy Originating in	Intended criteria for movements in			*Active enforcement agencies*
	General level of money wages	*Wage structure*	*Prices*	
I. 1945	Changes in cost of living only.	None: Uniform increases.	Rise in nonlabor costs and maintenance of absolute profit margins (1951–1953).	1) *Wages.* The parties (through Foundation of Labor) with active governmental intervention (through Board of Mediators) under authority of Extraordinary Decree. "Black Wages" outlawed. 2) *Prices.* Prior notification to Minister of Economic Affairs.
II. 1954	Maintenance of labor share in national income.	Differential rates of increase permitted.	1) None for wage increase up to 6% (1955–1956). 2) Where permitted, wage increases must not exceed 3%.	
III. 1959	In accordance with over-all increase in productivity.	Wage increases differentiated according to sectoral increases in productivity, up to a maximum.	1) As under I. 2) Prices to be cut where rates of productivity increase exceeded over-all average.	1) *Wages.* Extensive governmental intervention in collective bargaining and surveillance over prices. 2) *Prices. Ex post* notification of all price increases to Minister of Economic Affairs with some exceptions.
IV. 1963	To be established in semi-annual economic reports based on Central Plan projections of growth in output.	Individual industry-wide agreements to be consistent with agreed over-all increase in wage income.	1) (1966) As under I. 2) 5% of 1964 wage increase could be passed on. 3) But where the rate of return on capital falls below a specified level (4%, then 6%, then 7%), all wage increases could be passed on.	1) *Wages.* The parties, through the Foundation of Labor, although the wage target was to be based on official economic forecasts. The Board of Mediators retained standby powers to freeze wages and invalidate agreements. 2) *Prices.* Detailed governmental regulation of accounting and pricing, and inspection.

V. 1968–1969	No policy guidelines. (However, government continues attempts to restrain wage increases within limits based on projections of economic activity.)	Return to decentralized wage determination *de facto* (as well as formally) furnished basis for differentiation of wage increases.	Price freeze announced in April 1969, with provision for roll-back to levels in March except for increases in non-labor direct costs (including tax on value added).	1) *Wages*. Foundation participation in determination of central norm terminated. Prior approval of agreements by foundation, terminated by mutual consent. Power of Board of Mediators to review agreements likewise terminated. But minister retained ultimate power to invalidate agreements made under 1945 Decree. 2) *Prices*. Hope of legal backing under IV, but voluntary acceptance of *de facto* continuance. Control tightened in April 1969 and inspection staff increased.
VI. 1970	Over-all wage "freeze" of 7 per cent set for 1971, but employers permitted to pay lump sum up to $108 per worker to help settle strikes in 1970.			Passage of wage law formally empowering Minister of Social Affairs to declare specific collective agreements "non-binding" when negotiated increases are regarded as excessive in terms of over-all economic and social conditions, as well as to impose wage freezes for limited periods.

unaffiliated unions. Finally, and perhaps most important, the central union federations lack the formal constitutional controls over their affiliates possessed by the Swedish Federation of Labor.

The employers too are organized into political and sectarian associations. These differ from the union federations in being somewhat limited in jurisdiction; there are separate organizations in agriculture, in commerce, and in industry. Moreover, about 80 per cent of the employers in industry belong to the liberal nondenominational federation (CSWV), which, according to one study, "consequently can speak for Dutch employers more authoritatively than the largest of the union federations (the NVV) can speak for the labor movement."[3] Yet this employer association and the others stand in as marked contrast to the Swedish counterpart (which was empowered to take strikes and institute lockouts and to prevent members from doing so) as the Dutch union federations did with respect to their Swedish counterparts. Unlike the Swedish association, which is granted tight control over the lockout or strike decisions affecting its affiliates, the Dutch employers' associations have no control over their affiliated organizations or individual firms. Collective bargaining in both countries is conducted at the industry level, but in Holland, unlike Sweden, the industry bargains were not negotiated within an over-all "framework" established by the central union and employer federations.

It is true that in Holland, as in other countries where collective bargaining is formally decentralized, bargains set in some strategic sectors seem to influence powerfully the general movement of money-wage rates. In the

[3] William Fellner, *et al.*, *The Problem of Rising Prices* (Paris: OECD, 1961), p. 361.

Netherlands this pattern-setting role has been played by the settlements in the construction, steel, and metal fabricating industries, which employ more than a quarter of all Dutch unionists. On the other hand, the employer and union federations have engaged in explicit, *de facto* central bargaining since World War II, notwithstanding the decentralized nature of formal structures. They have done so because of their participation in and association with private and public bodies which have been assigned administrative functions in the succession of Dutch incomes policies. Thus, in the Netherlands, centralized bargaining was a result, rather than a precondition, of incomes policy. The British and others have insisted that the most important subobjective of incomes policy is to alter institutional behavior so as to reduce the degree of exploitation of disposable monopoly power. By this criterion Dutch incomes policy in the early postwar period was quite effective. That its effectiveness owed little to the preexisting structure of trade unionism is indicated by the fact that the independent unions expanded most rapidly in this period—a phenomenon attributed in good part to their lack of connection with the administrative apparatus of wage controls.

Government, quasi government, and politics.

Another hypothesis tested by early Dutch experience is that the existence of legal sanctions constitutes a necessary condition for the effectiveness of incomes policy. (The British "rogue elephant" theory, discussed in the preceding chapter, is one variant of this proposition.) Dutch experience does not cast doubt on this hypothesis (as it does on the strong hypothesis concerning structural centralization). It does, however, suggest that legal compulsion is not a sufficient condition of success; and it indicates that any system of legal sanctions must be rooted in a foundation of widespread and cooperative acceptance.

Faced with major problems of economic reconstruction at the end of World War II, the Dutch government secured passage of an Extraordinary Decree on Labor Relations in 1945, which included stringent powers of control over labor-market activity and wage determination. In addition to requiring governmental approval of any layoff or quit which might fail to secure consent of the parties—a provision which is still operative—the decree provided for enforcement of current official wage policy by a Board of Government Mediators which was empowered to review and either approve or disapprove collective contracts. Acting under this authority, the board proceeded to review draft agreements and to check their provisions for consistency with current governmental guidelines. Moreover, the decree made it illegal for employers to offer wages and other conditions of employment other than those thus approved by the Board of Mediators. A corps of wage inspectors was charged with enforcement, and, over the years, penalties in the form of fines and even imprisonment have been provided and, in some instances, exacted.

The board, however, drew its power not so much from legalistic sanctions as from the active involvement of the bargaining parties and other private-interest groups in the administration of wage policy. Appointments to the board have been designed to secure eminent representatives of the major political and religious organizations in the country, although this was not required by the decree. More importantly, the board depended on a close working relationship with the Foundation of Labor. This group had been established clandestinely by union and management leaders toward the end of the German occupation and has furnished the basis for employer-union cooperation ever since. The foundation initially desired wide but temporary power over all economic activity during the massive postwar reconstruction. It had to compromise on an advisory role in the determination of wages and other aspects of social policy. However, it proceeded to establish bipartisan subcommittees on wages, social insurance, job security issues, and related topics; and it became a powerful institution in connection with the determination and implementation of Dutch incomes policy.

Midway between the foundation and the governmental Board of Mediators, another institution was created—the Social and Economic Council (SEC). This is another advisory body, although with a broader charge than the foundation's, since it takes cognizance over all economic and social issues and is not restricted to incomes policy.[4] But it is an official body, with a third of its members appointed by the Crown, usually from academic and political life, while the remainder are divided between the employers' organizations and the union federations. In practice, the SEC ceded a major role in the administration of wage controls to the Foundation of Labor. The two institutions, however, are offshoots of a common underlying philosophy: that domestic problems, which cannot be resolved by the responses of private individuals under the stimulus of self-interest, ought to be dealt with, not by the state alone, but by "interest group activities."[5] In other words, according to this view, the absence of sufficiently competitive markets does *not*

[4] Wage policy was not viewed as the foremost concern of the council in its early years. For a more detailed description of the initial duties of the SEC, see Edelman and Fleming, *op. cit.*, pp. 226–230.

[5] For further elaboration, see J. Pen, "The Strange Adventures of Dutch Wage Policy," *British Journal of Industrial Relations*, November 1963, p. 320.

create the classic case for undiluted state intervention in modern society characterized by much private collective activity. (Another theory holds that public regulation of an industry is best performed by "a central representative agency.") The application of this philosophy, which we label "quasi government," to wage policy was carried to a more extreme form in Sweden, where the government has stood—or been held—aside from central wage determination, although on the understanding that the major private social partners "should produce results consistent with the public interest in economic stability and growth." The Swedes (following an unsuccessful episode in 1949) have been resolutely opposed to formal incomes policy and the Dutch have been equally resolute in its support (and pursuit); but both of these polar approaches have shared this common foundation of quasi government.

Reference should be made in this section to a further hypothesis partly tested by early Dutch experience. As a corollary of the wider proposition that union cooperation with incomes policy requires that the government of the day command the confidence of the unions, it is held that such cooperation will be forthcoming only if political parties closely allied to the dominant labor groups are in power. In the Netherlands, as elsewhere in Europe, this presumably means that an incomes policy dependent on union cooperation could succeed only if the Social Democrats are in office. It is true that the Socialists were in power in the Netherlands until 1959 and that during this period there occurred what some regard as one of the finest hours in the checkered history of incomes policy anywhere: the unions' agreement to a "wage stop" in 1951–1953, which implied a 5 per cent cut in real wages. They did so on the personal urging of an eminent economic planner, who was himself a Socialist and an influential figure in the incumbent regime. It is fruitless to speculate what might have occurred if some other party had been in office at the time; but the episode is widely believed to have reflected the influence of the strong ties which bound the NVV and the Socialist party together. On the other hand, the period during which the Socialists were in power considerably outlasted the honeymoon of incomes policy.

The preexistence of consensus; the importance of foreign trade.

Underlying the partnership between the government and the private parties and their joint review of collective agreements was a strong communal predisposition in favor of an effective incomes policy. That predisposition itself was only one facet of a strong feeling of national unity forged in common adversity. It originated, as indicated above, in wartime; and it was nourished by an appreciation of the magnitude of the task of postwar reconstruction in a small country whose high rate of population growth placed a premium on capital accumulation and whose heavy dependence on exports, which in Holland average 45 per cent of the gross national product, required that careful attention be paid to the level of labor costs. Thus, when it was estimated that the level of real wages was too high for balance-of-payments equilibrium, the response was an incomes policy designed to "restrict consumption" by restricting increases in money wages to increases in the cost of living, thereby having money wages trail behind productivity. This initial period of incomes policy covered the years 1945–1953 and culminated in the agreement to allow real wages actually to fall in response to a deficit in the balance of payments which emerged in 1951.

Thus this first phase illustrated the importance to

incomes policy of an actual or threatened balance-of-payments crisis, as a visible menace, of external origin, to the general welfare. Later experience, in the Netherlands and other countries, has reinforced this point and made it obvious. But the role of incomes policy as a concrete communal response to something generally accepted as a clear and present danger is limited. It is a question of show us the path and we will follow it although, as we shall see, the technical task of guidance is not negligible, and technical failure might dissipate the public's predisposition to guidance. However, proponents of incomes policy have claimed—or at least desired—more for it than furnishing guidance for the converted. The policy was itself supposed to generate consensus of a more enduring nature—to substitute restraint based on sophistication about some longer-term consequences of private group decisions for restraint based on a reflex reaction to visible crises. After a jet-assisted take-off (or even without one), the craft was supposed to fly on its own. It is to this problem of self-propulsion that the Dutch have been addressing themselves since the early 1950's, as the stock of exogenous assets which underwrote the effectiveness of their early incomes policy gradually depreciated.

EROSION OF THE EARLY BASES

Distributional problems.

In an economy characterized by a large private sector and also by a positive rate of growth in productivity, a policy of "consumption restriction" by constant (or restrained increase in) real wages implies a reduction in the share of wage income. If it was remarkable that the Dutch unions accepted this policy in 1951, it was not surprising that their patience was limited in duration.

Indeed, the policy of "consumption restriction" was never intended to be other than temporary; and in 1954 the Foundation of Labor requested that it be changed.

Another type of distributional problem concerned the industrial and occupational structure of wages. The Socialist tradition of egalitarianism was in part responsible for NVV support for a government-initiated interindustrial program of job evaluation in the early 1950's which was designed to secure an approximation to "equal pay for equal work," regardless of differences in the balance of supply and demand in various markets as well as anomalies rooted in historic developments. The realization of this objective required changes in the existing wage structures; but an incomes policy restricted in principle to the granting of cost-of-living increases generated uniform wage movements ("across the board"), and this aroused opposition in the NVV. The confessional federations were also impatient with the regime of uniform increases, but for reasons related to the distribution of income between aggregate wage income and profits, rather than to the distribution of wage income among industries and occupations. Pointing to the development of widespread interindustry variation in profit rates, they complained that existing policy did not permit them to obtain greater increases in high-profit industries. What they wanted in effect was a central policy which would maximize aggregate labor income through a system of discriminatory wage-setting. The resulting wage structure would presumably be different from the NVV model. On the other hand, to the extent that differences in "ability to pay" coincided with differences in labor demand, the maximizing model of these other labor groups more closely satisfied—in principle—the theoretical requirements of economic efficiency. Indeed, the employers were sympathetic to arguments raised on behalf of this position, for many of them were experiencing recruiting difficulties in the generally tight labor markets of the 1950's. It might be added that some provisions of the 1945 decree, under which the early system of uniform wage increases was administered, inhibited the shifting of resources into high-profit industries. Thus out of a diversity of motives and interests considerable pressure was built up in the 1950's for a new set of guidelines which might permit greater differentiation of wage increases.

The role of government.

By the end of the Korean War, Dutch employers were growing restive under the degree of government intervention which was associated with the administration of incomes policy under conditions of excess demand. The wage guidelines kept officially sanctioned wage levels below equilibrium rates, as they had been originally intended to do. This aggravated the recruiting problems referred to above, since in-migration of foreign labor was discouraged and, indeed, out-migration of skilled labor began to occur in the 1950's. Under the pressure of labor shortage, wages "drifted" above permissible guideline levels. Since drift was unlawful under the Extraordinary Decree of 1945, price inspectors were deployed to prevent the payment of "black wages," and prosecutions, fines, and even jail sentences ensued. The number of inspectors was too small to permit thoroughgoing enforcement, but the level of governmental intervention was sufficient to arouse active employer hostility. Recourse to governmental intervention, employer resistance to it, and the growing inability to hold wage increases within the guidelines signified a significant weakening of voluntary restraint and indicated the need to devise viable alternatives to the stimulus provided by postwar reconstruction.

Collective bargaining with a postwar work force.

The willingness of employers to grant wage increases above the guideline began to undermine collective bargaining at the level of the industry and the firm. This left the unions with no real bargaining tasks to perform for their members, since it was no achievement to negotiate the "maximum" permissible wage increase. Had the membership remained willing to dispense with hard bargaining, this would not necessarily have threatened the position of organized labor; it would merely have induced a redistribution of power and prestige within the movement, away from the traditionally autonomous affiliated unions and toward the central bodies which "negotiated" the central guidelines. But two episodes in the mid-fifties indicate that, while leadership at the federation level (at least in the NVV) was willing to accept guidelines at excess-demand levels, the membership was not, and that, in consequence, incomes policy strained the institutional fabric of the Dutch labor movement.

The first episode occurred in 1955 when the union leadership agreed to an increase of only 3 per cent (consisting entirely of fringe benefit improvements) at the government's behest, despite the prevalence of high internal demand and a strong balance-of-payments position. For the first time many union members criticized their leaders for supporting official guidelines. The second episode occurred in 1957. With wages rising at an annual rate of 8–9 per cent and a balance-of-payments crisis developing, the unions again accepted a policy of extreme restraint. As in 1951–1953, their willingness to accept a reduction in real wages and a rise in unemployment could be "justified" by the presence of visible external danger to the economy; moreover, profits were also to be reduced. But in 1955–1957, the leadership could not carry the membership with them; pressure for a return to decentralized bargaining began to build up.[6]

Thus much of the Spirit of '45 had evaporated with a return to more normal peacetime conditions. Moreover, with the passage of a decade, the ranks of working veterans of the wartime occupation had begun to thin out. They were increasingly replenished by younger workers with shorter memories and markedly weaker allegiance to the Socialist and religious creeds which still motivated the older generation whose representatives continued to occupy key positions in the central leadership. The emergence of a generation gap within the Dutch labor movement was reflected in lagging membership; it is significant that the most rapidly expanding unions were those independent organizations which were not affiliated with the central federations and were not part of the quasi-governmental apparatus which was so important in the formulation and administration of the incomes policy. This fact of demographic life alone has made it imperative to replace some of the original bases of Dutch incomes policy with new constructions capable of tapping different sources of grass-root support.

NEW CONSTRUCTIONS

Productivity and distributional criteria for wage and price behavior; 1954–1959: "Welfare" wage rounds.

In 1954 the policy was changed, at the request of the Foundation of Labor, to permit advances in real wages, to prevent labor's share in the national income from

[6] See Windmuller, *op. cit.*, pp. 351–354.

declining, and to permit intersectoral variation of wage increases. Accordingly, the government's guidelines allowed money wage increases to exceed permissible price increases. Moreover, the wage guidelines were intended to serve as *maxima,* which the unions would not be able to negotiate in all sectors; thus the condition of differentiation would be satisfied. In practice, however, demand conditions were such that the maximum could always be reached, while the foundation or the Board of Mediators disallowed settlements in excess of the maximum. Thus wage increases continued to be uniform across sectors. The unions complained about this and also claimed that the share of wages in the national income had fallen. As a result, the Foundation of Labor failed to function effectively, and, in 1955–1956, the government was forced to resort to arbitration. The government also tried to reinvigorate the policy of differentiated wage incomes by price controls: the new policy required that wage increases in excess of 3 per cent and up to 6 per cent come out of profits; no price increases would be allowed to cover such increases in labor costs. But this attempt, as we know, failed, as wages and prices generally soared above guideline rates and a balance-of-payments crisis developed.

1959–1963: Sectoral productivity guideline.

Between 1959 and 1963, the government attempted to resolve the difficulties emerging under the old policy by permitting greater differentiation of wage increases and, in principle, a greater role for collective bargaining at the industry level. In 1959 the Labor government was replaced by a more conservative Liberal government which at times espoused the greater freedom in wage determination advocated by the employer constituency. The new policy provided for wage increases in accordance with movements in sectoral labor productivity, although industries with the highest productivity trends were asked to combine modest wage increases with price cuts, while those with the lowest productivity trends were to be permitted wage increases in excess of the sectoral productivity trend along with a price increase. This condition was supposed to rule out the development of excessive and drift-inducing occupational wage anomalies and to contribute directly to over-all price stability. (It is similar to the exceptions in the *U.S. Guideposts.* Both policies in principle satisfied the requirements of over-all price stability. Their major criteria were, however, opposed. The Dutch policy contemplated the differentiation of wage increases in accordance with sectoral differences in productivity growth; all prices [with the exceptions noted above] were to remain stable. American policy, as a general rule, contemplated uniform wage increases in accordance with variations in over-all productivity growth.)

On the pricing side, the 1961 Law on Prices replaced a 1939 statute empowering the government to impose price stops. Although the new law permitted the imposition of maximum prices by the government, its main contribution was to specify a set of criteria for pricing decisions. The main features (some of which had been foreshadowed in the 1955–1956 emergency) were: (1) price increases were only justified by increases in *nonwage* costs; (2) prices were to be limited to maintaining the *absolute* profit margin.

The new wage policy ran into difficulty almost immediately. In the first place, it had a weak theoretical basis, which did not acknowledge any role for interoccupational or interindustrial wage differences in the face of different market conditions. Secondly, the data on sectoral productivity movements were poor; and, in practice, the parties bargained over the productivity statistics needed to justify wage increases. Finally, weekly hours were supposed to be reduced from 48 to 45 in three years, but in the event, most firms provided the full reduction in 1960, thus accelerating hourly wage costs. On the price side, while the firms agreed to notify the Minister of Economic Affairs of price increases, such notification was shifted from an *ex ante* to an *ex post* basis, except for some food staples and fuel.

1963–1967: Guidelines from the Central Plan.

In 1963, the policy was changed again. Productivity was dropped as an explicit criterion for money wage increases. Instead, *ex ante* wage targets were obtained from projections of the Central Planning Bureau's econometric model of the Netherlands. The Social and Economic Council (SEC) was to promulgate these targets in semi-annual economic reports, which might provide rough quantitative indications of the "permissible" increase in labor costs.

This approach, however, involved the exchange of one set of statistical difficulties for another, which in fact sentenced the new policy to almost instant death. The difficulties started with a badly pessimistic forecast for 1963 from the Central Planning Bureau, which implied that the permissible wage increase was 1.2 per cent. The SEC, recognizing the probable attitude of the negotiating parties to this guideline, suggested that an additional and arbitrary 1.5 per cent was tolerable, so that the total "permissible" wage increase was 2.7 per cent. Even so, employers openly announced their intention to pay more than the guideline increase; and payment of black wages was widespread. Moreover, rank-and-file pressures developed to the point where strikes, normally a rarity in Dutch industrial relations, appeared to be imminent in several industries. As a result, the foundation had to supplement its original target increase of 2.7 per cent with an increment of 10 per cent (half of which was to reduce the gap between actual and contractual wages and the rest to reduce the alleged wage gap vis-à-vis other countries). In the event, wages and salaries rose by about 13 per cent in 1963, 15 per cent in 1964, and 11 per cent in 1965.[7]

This episode reinforced the union criticism—raised also in the United Kingdom, Sweden, and Germany—that government forecasts tend to be biased conservatively and can cause wage-price policy marginally to distribute income away from wages or to increase wage drift and thus undermine the position of the unions with respect to their constituents. The latter occurred in 1963 and 1964, and the parties in the foundation were unable to reach agreement on wage guidelines in 1966 and 1967. The SEC, the official advisory body on wage policy, was also severely split, with one faction favoring total abolition of controls. The government stepped in and announced a wage norm of 7½ per cent and the unions and the nonconfessional employers' association refused to participate in the policy any longer. By the autumn of 1967 all factions within the Foundation of Labor had

[7]The OECD examined and rejected several economic hypotheses concerning the cause of the wage explosion. The report concluded that institutional factors, including employer impatience with complicated rules, the domination of employer associations by firms most able to pay higher wages and rank-and-file pressures on union leadership, were responsible for the timing of the explosion. See OECD Economic Surveys, *Netherlands,* July, 1966, p. 16.

united in opposition to the system of wage restraint which had been adopted in 1963. The unions insisted on the elimination of central guidelines, claiming that experience in the first half of the decade showed that such guidelines tended to be exceeded by employers and to serve as *minimum* targets, rather than a ceiling, for unions, especially in periods of very high employment. The government concurred, and thus wage determination under decentralized collective bargaining without a fixed over-all norm was sanctioned as normal procedure in the Netherlands in 1968, for the first time since the end of World War II.

On the other hand, the union federations did not insist on absolute laissez-faire as a matter of principle. They explicitly agreed that the government should have emergency powers to freeze wages across the board. Thus they were still willing to recognize the need for incomes policy as an *ad hoc* response to clear and present danger; but they had lost faith—at least for the time being—in its educational efficacy as a modifier of worker attitudes and day-to-day institutional behavior. In retrospect it might appear that a policy based on wage norms which changed rapidly in accordance with variations in the near-term economic outlook stood little chance of accomplishing such fundamental change, even in the absence of forecasting error. As things developed, the abandonment in 1963 of emphasis on past movements in productivity as a determinant of the wage norm was followed in 1967 by the disappearance of the norm itself.

The role of government.

Attempts to develop criteria for wage and price behavior under which sufficient voluntary restraint could be elicited were mirrored in attempts to devise methods of administration which might minimize the role of government. The policy of "permissive," differentiated wage increases adopted in 1954 was in part a response to employer objections to the degree of governmental determination associated with the earlier policy of "consumption restriction." In fact, as we know, permissiveness did not generate differentiation. The latter appeared to require the enforcement of a price policy which denied price increases in response to increases in labor costs. This approach failed in 1956, but it was tried again in 1959 when it was combined with the wage policy based on (differing) trends in sectoral productivity. The price policy, which was written into law, required that firms notify the Minister of Economic Affairs in advance of contemplated price increases; and the Law on Prices (1961) was to be enforced by the Economic Control Office, with a staff of two hundred price controllers. As far as the wage policy was concerned, the Board of Mediators retained its power to review proposed contracts and was specifically charged with the task of reducing excessive wage increases and also of requesting price reductions in sectors with the highest growth in productivity. Nevertheless, this policy, which was introduced by a conservative government (of Liberals and Clericals), was viewed as permitting more freedom for collective bargaining at the industry level than the original, centralized policy had done. It is pertinent to recall that the Board of Mediators, although armed with governmental sanctions under the decree of 1945, was an independent body, composed of representatives of private interests, and not a governmental agency.

However, when the new policy failed to yield objective guidelines and when collective bargaining took the form of negotiating over the productivity data to serve as the basis for wage increases, the government issued a series of directives to the board and the negotiating parties which purported to clarify the application of the policy. This was the first serious challenge to the board's autonomy in the postwar period and resulted in dissatisfaction among both board members and some union and employer leaders over interference in what had been a smoothly operating review procedure. Moreover, in successive years the government directives came to take the form of highly detailed formulae, which were supposed to specify the permissible amounts of sectoral wage increases, so that in the end the scope of discretion left to collective bargaining was no greater than before. The 1959 policy was, therefore, a failure. It did not have the desired economic effect, and although introduced in response to demands for greater negotiating freedom in wage determination, it achieved more detailed government regulation and enforcement, thereby reducing even further the support of the parties for government wage policy.

The next change in policy, in 1963, although reviving the central wage norm and dropping the productivity criteria, sought directly to remove the government from intervention in collective bargaining. Instead of relying on the alleged self-enforcing qualities of a set of criteria, it sought to make the central union federations and employer associations responsible for policy execution. This was done by shifting primary administrative authority from the Board of Mediators to the Foundation of Labor, on which only the private federations are represented.

Under the 1963 policy, the foundation was to hold a prior discussion with the government about an appropriate national wage target, based on semiannual economic reports by the Social and Economic Council (which in turn drew on forecasts by the Central Planning Bureau). After consultation with the individual unions in the various industries, the union federations and the employer groups in the Foundation were to hold discussions to determine specific industry guidelines consistent with the national target and subsequently attempt to persuade their affiliates to abide by these guidelines in the collective agreements signed at the industry level. The latter now required approval by the foundation rather than the Board of Mediators, although copies of draft agreements had to be sent to the board. The latter could intervene and possibly declare a contract "nonbinding," but only if the foundation's members were deadlocked. The government retained power to call a short-term wage freeze (of one or two months) or to authorize the board to issue general wage directives and approve all agreements—but only in cases where it failed to reach agreement with the foundation about a wage target, which could presumably occur only in some economic emergency.

Although the new policy relegated the government to a supporting role, a governmental agency, the Central Planning Bureau, received a good share of blame for the policy's stillbirth. The criticism that wage norms based on official forecasts of economic activity tend to be conservatively biased is generally acknowledged to have had some merit, at least in this instance. The foundation, as we have seen, tried to preserve its new central role in policy-making by ratifying the actual wage increases after the fact. However, the strain involved in attempting to administer an incomes policy at a time of severe internal demand pressures increased the level of conflict and tensions within an institution that had been designed for the purpose of proposing—rather than administering—policy. Moreover, union leadership at the federation level came under increasing strain as neither its own rank and file nor the employers supported the policy of restraint which it was trying to administer. In July 1965, the three labor federations proposed the elimination of all review procedures. Neither the government nor the employers were at first prepared to accept this position, and proposed alternative procedures aimed at salvaging such key elements of the 1963 system as the central norm and participation by the foundation in the bargaining process.[8] These proposals, however, were rejected by the NVV; and, after the foundation and the Social and Economic Council deadlocked in 1966 and 1967 and the government announced its own norm, the other parties agreed to terminate the attempt at a privately run wage policy. The unions and the nonconfessional employers' association announced that the foundation would revert to its former role as the locus for joint consideration of general labor problems.

The breakdown of the foundation did not, however, spell the end of all voluntary participation. Although the legal price controls enacted in 1961 formally lapsed at the end of 1966, the employers volunteered to extend the policy and emphasized that wage increases would not be passed on into price increases. In 1967, the Minister of Economic Affairs induced some branches of industry to cut prices; a general price freeze was instituted; and the staff of price controllers was increased. But business support soon waned, and prices began to rise rapidly. On April 8, 1969, another price freeze was announced.

[8] For example, in 1965 the Minister of Social Affairs proposed that the foundation establish informal agreements on wage increases in a few of the leading sectors. Management favored giving the Board of Mediators authority to delay new agreements up to four weeks and using wage criteria based on the SEC reports. The latter, however, would not be explicit figures derived from the Central Planning Bureau projections.

Prices were to be cut back to the levels of March 14. They were to be recalculated on the basis of October first of that year, with increases allowed to absorb such increases in costs as were accounted for by the value-added tax, but not by wage increases. The failure of wage policy placed the burden of restraint on a stringent system of price controls.

It was not intended that way, for the government accompanied the price controls by a vigorous attempt to control wages as well. The 1963 policy did provide for intervention by the government and the Board of Mediators in the event of a deadlock in the foundation; the government did restore to the board power to approve, delay, and suspend wage increases; and the Board, armed with the official wage norm of 7½ per cent, proceeded to reject contracts covering over a half million employees which called for increases averaging 10½ per cent.[9] Moreover, although the new phase of policy, which began in 1968, was described as "free," the board was still permitted to "advise" the Minister of Social Affairs to declare agreements nonbinding if they were believed to threaten aggregate economic stability. The minister might then request the opinion of a new five-member Wage Advisory Committee (chaired by the vice chairman of the Board of Mediators).

Nevertheless, the new policy commanded the support of the private parties at the outset. It dispensed with the central norm; it permitted decentralized bargaining and variation in wage increases; it removed the major source of strain and internal dissension within the Foundation of Labor. But such negative virtues did not suffice for the government. It perforce was primarily interested in

[9]OECD Economic Surveys, *Netherlands* (Paris: OECD, April 1967), p. 39.

results, by which it meant holding wage increases down to a steady annual rate of 6.5 per cent until 1971. However, compensation for reductions in the work week—currently a general European phenomenon—ran negotiated increases up to an average of 9 per cent. So, in March 1968, less than three months after the start of the new policy, the minister asked the foundation to restrict the reduction in the workweek to 1/4 hour per day in 1968 and in 1969. The foundation rejected this request as inconsistent with the principle of free wage determination. After securing advice from the new Wage Advisory Commission, the minister then unbound three agreements, including one in construction, which called for a reduction in the workweek of half an hour; and in May the government proposed to the parliament that all collective agreements be frozen through 1969. However, union protest was sufficiently strong to induce the government to withdraw its proposal from parliament. As a sequel, when the 1969 shipbuilding and engineering industries settled for $6\frac{1}{2}$ per cent at the beginning of 1969—thereby exceeding the government's own target of 4 per cent—the Advisory Commission unanimously reversed itself and advised the Cabinet that the Minister of Social Affairs should not use his power to invalidate these agreements! The government proceeded to adopt a deflationary policy.

Thus the unions, having virtuously refused once again to re-assume responsibility for formulating general wage policy, prevented the Liberal government from invoking the only restraints provided for in the new policy. The legal basis for these restraints remained the Extraordinary Decree of 1945, but, in view of the union challenges, the government, in September 1968, decided to introduce more permanent legislation. The proposed new wage law, while affirming free collective bargaining as a basic principle, provided that the government have formal authority to:

1) Declare collective agreements nonbinding (or invalid), in the interest of general social and economic conditions. This would be done by the Minister of Social Affairs, after consultation with the Wage Advisory Commission.

2) Extend wage agreements or freeze wages, in special circumstances, but only for a maximum period of six months and only after consultation with the Social and Economic Council and the Foundation of Labor, as well as the Wage Advisory Commission. The government felt that this power was necessary because collective agreements had recently been specifying only minimum —rather than actual—wage rates, which individual employers were free to supplement with local "drift" increments. A wage freeze means that the onus is on employers not to raise wages outside collective negotiations, as well as through such negotiations.

3) As a last resort, require approval of all collective agreements by the Board of Government Mediators. This power would have to be confirmed by parliament within three months after introduction. Moreover, it could last for only one year and would only be invoked in periods of acute crisis, such as the combination of high unemployment and a serious balance-of-payments deficit.

This measure was strongly opposed by the NVV, who were supported in parliament by the Socialists. The NVV was particularly opposed to the formalizing of power to nullify collective agreements, partly because the Minister of Social Affairs indicated that he might nullify even minor contracts on the grounds that they could prove to be pattern setters. They also opposed the first provision, because, under its terms, the minister would not have to consult the Social and Economic Council (where the negotiating parties are represented) before invalidating agreements. They were further opposed to a formal reintroduction of the intrusive role of the government mediators, and in this objection they were joined by the employer federations and the SEC. Finally, although the NVV never objected to a governmental freeze in response to a balance-of-payments crisis, it was suspicious of the more vague and general language used in the first provision summarized above.

While the law was being debated, the tripartite Social and Economic Council was able to announce agreement on a wage norm in 1970. This "Agreement of June 1969," however, was made very precarious by union opposition to the wage law. Debate was so intense that the issue seemed to threaten the stability of the liberal Coalition government. The measure was finally passed (in 1970) with some minor amendments. However, the Socialist and Catholic federations (NVV and NKV) announced that they were withdrawing from the Social and Economic Council and from central bargaining; and the Minister of Social Affairs was warned that parliament had granted him nothing more than a "paper sword."

In fact, the debate involved a good deal of shadow-boxing. The formal grant of power sought by the government amounted to little more than it already had acquired through past enactments and precedent. The NVV had always accepted the need for emergency controls; and, while it had opposed the inclusion among such controls of intervention in specific agreements, the unions had demonstrated their capacity to oppose this type of intervention so convincingly that it seemed they had little to fear from legal enactment. As one writer had observed, "Such intervention does not work when the labor market is already tense. The power of the minister does not suffice when he is not supported in his policy by employers, employees, and their organizations."[10]

This hypothesis, forged out of the shipbuilding and engineering episodes in 1969, won speedy reconfirmation after passage of the new law. The engineering contract for 1970 and 1971 occasioned concern in the government because it contained a sliding scale based on increases in both cost of living and productivity. If this set the pattern, it would raise unit labor costs by 8 per cent in 1970, whereas the official maximum was pegged at only 7 per cent for that year and the government was trying to damp down the wage-price spiral. Nevertheless, the Minister of Social Affairs persuaded the Cabinet that he ought not test his newly legislated legal powers in this instance. Yet the Central Economic Plan was warning against the inflationary consequences of linking wage increases to price increases; and the Minister of Economic Affairs resigned in disappointment.[11]

Thus the sixties witnessed the collapse of an ambitious attempt at a privately run incomes policy; whereas the seventies at the outset revealed the severe limitations of a policy based on legal compulsion, especially under conditions of excess demand. In light of the strains to which both types of policy have subjected some of the country's major institutions, these failures are readily understandable. Less understandable is the apparent reluctance of

[10] W. Albeda, in *Economisch-Statistiche Berichten,* 1 October 1969.

[11] *The Economist,* January 10, 1970, pp. 59–61.

the various elements in Dutch society to give up on incomes policy.

THE ECONOMIC RATIONALE

One reason why the search for new policy bases continues unabated, is the belief, widely held, that, in principle, incomes policy is a highly desirable instrument in the small, open Dutch economy and that in practice the policy has not been ineffective in terms of its major economic objectives. The potential usefulness of an incomes policy is suggested by the following equation, based on annual data for 1954–1968:

$$\dot{W} = .0115 + \underset{(3.24)}{.025\, U^{-2}} + \underset{(6.53)}{1.39\, \dot{P}} \qquad R^2 = .829$$

In this equation $\dot{W}$ is the rate of change of the hourly wage rate in industry, U is the registered unemployment rate, $\dot{P}$ is the rate of change of consumer prices, and the t statistics are in parentheses. Attempts to reduce $\dot{W}$ by raising U would represent classic deflationary policy, whereas attempts to reduce $\dot{W}$ by restraining $\dot{P}$ would represent one form of incomes policy. Our unemployment coefficient is consistent with the UN study's classification of the Netherlands among the countries with "high sensitivity" of wages to changes in the unemployment level,[12] which implies that inflation could be checked without treading too heavily on the fiscal-monetary brakes. On the other hand, the Netherlands is also classified as a "low unemployment" country; during this period unemployment has ranged from under 1 per

[12] U.N. Economic Commission for Europe, *Incomes in Post-War Europe* (Geneva: Economic Commission for Europe, 1967), Chapter 3, p. 14.

cent to a high of 2¼ per cent during the 1958 recession (and these rates probably understate the amount of unemployment that would be observed under the U.S. system). This persistence of below-average unemployment indicates the depth of commitment to high-employment policies and, therefore, the extent of distaste for reliance on deflation to dampen inflationary tendencies. This aversion is further reflected in the fact that, during 1964–1968 – after the collapse of the incomes policy based on the Foundation of Labor – the rate of price increase in the Netherlands (4.4 per cent per annum) was exceeded only in Japan, among the ten leading industrial nations in the Organization for Economic Cooperation and Development (OECD).

Thus the magnitude of the price change coefficient in the cited equation might hold considerable interest for policy makers. The implication that, at a given (and low) level of unemployment a decline of one percentage point in the rate of price increase would be promptly translated into a decline well in excess of one percentage point in the rate of increase in money wage rates, at least makes understandable the reliance on direct price restraint as a continuing element in Dutch incomes policy, even after the failure of the wage policy in 1964.

On the other hand, the equation exaggerates the potential indirect effectiveness of a policy of price restraint, because the wage data on which it is based refer to wage rates and not earnings. This means that wage drift is excluded from the dependent variable; and drift in the Netherlands seems to be "chiefly 'compensatory,' in the sense that a relatively large increase in conventional rates in a given year is most often accompanied by a relatively small amount of drift (and vice versa)."[13] Thus the

[13] *Ibid.*, p. 22.

estimated amount of black wages declined considerably following the 1964 wage explosion.[14] This offset relationship suggests that price restraint would be less effective in reducing the rate of increase in earnings – and therefore total labor costs – than in rates, although it should be recalled that such a policy would itself offer no incentive to employers to raise the demand price of labor. On the other hand, evidence on the compensatory nature of drift does suggest that the most heavily stressed component of Dutch incomes policy – direct restraint on wages – has failed to generate any beneficial long-term, structural change in the trade-off relationship between unemployment and the rate of change in hourly labor costs. This is consistent with evidence of institutional strain generated by incomes policy.

Yet failure to modify structural economic relationships and the underlying institutional forms and behavior does not exclude all possibility of economic effectiveness. The policy, it is sometimes maintained, could nevertheless succeed in depressing the *relative levels* (as contrasted with rates of change) of Dutch costs and prices. This was the task originally assigned to Dutch incomes policy, and in some quarters it is maintained that this task was performed effectively up to the mid-1960's, when the wage explosion occurred. That phenomenon indeed is cited in this connection: the events associated with the policy's breakdown are taken as evidence of its prior effectiveness. Other exhibits offered as evidence of a depressed level of labor costs were: a rising share of exports to the main manufacturing countries, a cumulative net surplus on current account, and some loss of labor to West Germany. The persistence of relatively low

[14] OECD Economic Surveys, *Netherlands* (Paris: OECD, July 1966).

levels of unemployment and tight labor markets is also consistent with this hypothesis. The role of black wages, however, is not so readily assimilated, unless, possibly, it be maintained that the level of black wages (as well as the level of wage rates) was suppressed by the effectiveness of direct price restraint.[15] Moreover, the hypothesis that Dutch labor costs were relatively low is also understandable in the light of a relatively strong trend in Dutch productivity as well as the maintenance of an undervalued currency. The former is another phenomenon to which price control might have contributed via a squeeze on profit margins—but only marginally—and only if wages were not effectively restrained in the first instance.

Indeed, consideration of the behavior of the Dutch balance of payments after the early 1960's would seem, superficially at least, to strengthen the role attributed to productivity and to weaken the case for incomes policy. For the policy's collapse and the wage explosion in 1963–1964 were not reflected in a balance-of-payments crisis. The wage increases were partly offset by strong increases in productivity and by rising consumer prices which, together with an initial decline in the marginal propensity to consume, held down the rise in consumption. As a result, both exports and domestic investment were able to rise strongly. By 1966, exports began to decline, the Netherlands swung to a net import position, and the authorities permitted some deflation which was effective in reducing inflationary pressures. In the first half of 1967, an export-led recovery in output was asso-

[15] An OECD account maintained that the importance of black wages had declined in 1964. This point was offered in opposition to the position that the ensuing explosion was purely a phenomenon of excess demand. But, by the same token, it could presumably be regarded as evidence of prior policy effectiveness in suppressing latent cost-push tendencies. See OECD Economic Surveys, *Netherlands* (Paris: OECD, July 1966).

ciated with a rise in unemployment—to 2.5 per cent—and for the first time since 1960, the number of unemployed exceeded the number of job vacancies. But the balance-of-payments position improved despite a slowdown in the rise in world trade. In 1968–1969, expansion was rapid and associated with a high rate of wage and price inflation, which stimulated the government's abortive attempts at control. Imports rose more rapidly than exports for a while, but the latter continued strongly despite the very high rate of domestic inflation, so that in the first half of 1970 the current account returned to surplus. What price incomes policy now?

THE FUTURE OF DUTCH INCOMES POLICY: A HIGHER COST-BENEFIT RATIO?

The Central Economic Plan for 1970, in discussing the absence of surplus on current account in 1969, observed that "one has been attaching less and less significance to this indicator . . . one is less quick nowadays to bring up 'our competitive position.'" Indeed, when the unions had been criticized for failing to agree on a wage norm in 1966 and 1967, they pointed to the country's satisfactory balance-of-payments position by way of minimizing the loss of this policy instrument. But the rise in consumer prices had become so rapid by the last quarter of 1969—at an annual rate of 7.5 per cent—that public unrest seemed to qualify the achievement of more price stability as an objective in its own right. And the leadership of the NVV came to the conclusion that their bargaining affiliates were ready to accept some restraint.

On the other hand, the unions had lost 16,000 members between 1967 and 1968;[16] and, as noted above, the

[16] U.S. Bureau of Labor Statistics, *Labor Developments Abroad,* May 1969, p. 1.

younger workers—a growing proportion of whom were in white-collar occupations—had been questioning union cooperation in a government policy designed to hold down wages. The problem was aggravated by the passage of a minimum-wage law in 1965, as a result of which minimum wages came to about 70 per cent of the average wage. This disaffected some of the more highly paid skilled workers.[17] All this means that the cost to the unions of supporting an incomes policy has been increasing. Moreover, the young and the nonmanual employees—whose growing ranks have accounted for a substantial change in the political complexion as well as in the demographic composition of Holland's work force—are much more loosely bound than their fathers to the ideological and confessional ties which have connected unions to political parties and hence to governmental policy-making. This weakening of political ties should imply a diminution of the differences which have historically separated the three union federations; and in 1967 they formed a common executive to plan a joint action program. In 1969, the chairman of the NVV, although a Socialist member of parliament, declared that he was not married to that party but was more interested in the new political movement of "progressive concentration." The latter has generated a new political party, the "Political Party Radicals" whose constituency is drawn from the various confessional parties. This blurring of political and ideological divisions might, as in Italy, produce a trade-union movement united by a common dedication to pork chops, American style. But this

[17] In the United States, skilled workers have rebelled against egalitarian wage policies by exerting political pressure within their national unions, but this course of action was almost dictated by U.S. labor law, which makes it difficult for small groups to break out of established bargaining units. In Holland, on the other hand, workers simply quit or fail to join unions.

weakening of traditional political loyalties at the same time implies a decline in the willingness of union groups to assume the costs of supporting policies calling for private abstinence in the public interest—even as those costs themselves are increasing.

The unions, therefore, have served notice that some of this added burden must be shifted to the government, as official sponsor of any incomes policy, and to the public itself, as the presumptive beneficiary of such policy. They have done so in a variety of ways, some of which were revealed with the publication of the fragile agreement of June 1969.

In the first place, that agreement specified a wage norm which called for a rise of 2.5 to 3 per cent in real, not money, terms. This implied more complete compensation for increases in the cost of living. Whereas past agreements provided for maximum compensation only after a rise of one percentage point in the consumer price index—and then only for a rise of two additional points—the NVV conditioned an offer to restrict an increase in the basic money wage to 5 per cent on the guarantee of compensation for any rise in prices in excess of the estimated 2.5 per cent. This would immunize the unions against conservatively biased official forecasts, but the principle was also enshrined in the engineering agreements which caused such concern in planning and cabinet circles. Nevertheless, top union officials feel that they must guarantee their members a *quid pro quo* in the form of a larger rise in their real wages under incomes policy than had occurred in its absence.

The idea that the policy should have something specific in it for the people who are asked to accept restraint coincides with the opinion of some German experts who feel that incomes policy might stand a better chance in

Germany if the government offered the unions large wage increases in the early part of the upswing in exchange for restraint later on. Moreover, to the extent that acceptance of this proposal would improve the distribution of income from the viewpoint of the wage earner, it would accord with the factors making for what the Dutch regard as a highly egalitarian distribution of income. Many officials regard this as the best protection against the sort of anarchistic unrest and disruption which has been plaguing industrial relations and economies in Germany, Italy, and France.

In the second place, the unions conditioned acceptance of the June agreement on the government's willingness to forego an increase in the value-added tax, which would presumably be passed along in the form of price increases. The budget which subsequently appeared in fact did provide for such an increase.

In the third place, their intense opposition to the passage of the wage law at this time made it clear that the unions were not willing to support an incomes policy which contemplated detailed governmental intervention in decentralized collective-bargaining activities. They were willing, as we know, to grant the government authority to declare a general freeze on wages—and other incomes as well. (So would the AFL-CIO in the U.S., for this would throw the onus of responsibility on the government, as far as the unions and their members are concerned.) However, the formal passage of the act would probably not constitute an insuperable obstacle to the resumption of central negotiations, provided that the provisions for detailed intervention are allowed to remain a dead letter.

Finally, the interest shown by Dutch union leaders in some forms of worker participation should be given brief mention in this context. They are: (1) "capital-growth sharing," whereby a share of "surplus" profits (after deduction of depreciation, taxes, interest, and an amount for "reasonable" dividends) would be diverted to employees—of the enterprise or in the industry or economy-wide; (2) "investment pay," an "additional" wage increase which could not be spent for at least five years; and (3) union representation equal to shareholder representation on company boards of directors, in accordance with some changes in corporate law which were in fact recommended by the Social and Economic Council in 1969. The interest of the NVV and the NKV in profit-sharing dates from the early 1950's and their consequent frustration by the role allegedly played by corporate internal financing in increasing the inequality in the distribution of wealth. However, in more recent years, the main underlying motive of the union federations in championing these changes has been to provide the young, bored, disillusioned, and restless workers with incentives to participate more directly in the private policy-making which affects their economic destinies and with a mechanism for such "participation." By implementing such changes through collective bargaining, unions might find vital replacements for old, played-out claims on the affections and loyalties of the Dutch wage earners, but the interests of the employers and the public would also be served if absenteeism and turnover could be reduced and if the Netherlands could be spared the epidemic of wildcat striking which has swept through so much of Europe. In addition, the Dutch unionists have pointed to certain presumptive anti-inflationary properties of the first two innovations:

It is believed that some of the conflicts of interest, and "powerful influences behind the scenes" will disappear or be significantly reduced by a redistribution which is seen as a step towards a more democratic society. More specifically, if workers are given some say in the level of investment and its allocation, as would result from the creation of the special Funds to manage the workers' savings, they would tend to adopt a more "responsible" attitude to such things as the role of the general interest in the disposition of aggregate resources, including, perhaps, the need for restraint in increases in consumption of certain items.[18]

More specifically still, it has been claimed that, since capital-growth sharing would in effect be a private tax on profits, it would not induce compensatory price increases; but any wage increases in excess of a norm established under incomes policy could be made to take the form of blocked investment pay. Thus these innovations might reconcile the sociopolitical objectives of "participation" not only with organizational needs of the trade unions and the requirements of economic growth but with price stability as well. It would be beyond the scope of this analysis to attempt to pass careful judgment on these *a priori* claims which are so clearly merited by the issues. It is relevant to our purpose, however, to point out that costs as well as benefits would be associated with measures looking toward redistribution of wealth and power, because to the extent that the revival of incomes policy is associated with these measures, the costs which they entail must be set off against the benefits yielded by incomes policy. Indeed, to the extent that any participatory policy requires and obtains a greater degree of decentralization in institutional structure[19] and decision-making, it tends to reduce the potential administrative effectiveness of incomes policy.

[18] D. Robinson and S. Barkin, *Workers' Negotiated Savings Plans for Capital Formation,* Regional Trade Union Seminar, Final Report, Organization for Economic Co-Operation and Development, Manpower and Social Affairs Directorate (Paris: 1970), p. 27.

[19] Thus the OECD study cited above notes that the Dutch union movement not only insisted that capital-growth sharing and investment pay be implemented through collective bargaining but that it

Thus, in their search for new bases of support not only for incomes policy but also for their own organizations, the trade unionists in the Netherlands have recently appeared to set up a number of positive and negative conditions for acceptance. Some of these conditions would in themselves limit the administrative effectiveness of the policy; others would place a heavier economic burden on it by denying to the government recourse to certain deflationary alternatives; still others would, at least in principle, entail some redistribution of wealth and power which might affect the performance of the economy and would definitely increase the degree of uncertainty with which the policy maker must cope. In the absence of the negative stimulus to compliance generated in the past by threatened or actual crisis in the balance of payments, the cost of incomes policy has gone up. The policy maker can no longer regard incomes policy as virtually costless or riskless in political or economic (efficiency) terms. Nor, at least under the conditions outlined above, can he count on as extensive recourse to deflationary measures in the presence of an ineffectual incomes policy as he could in the absence of any such policy at all.

---

had a marked preference for one large national fund "for the former." "But they also recognize," it continues, "that this may not be possible." (*Ibid.*, p. 78.) Indeed, the requirements of "participation" would mitigate against this outcome, which, in addition to yielding a more egalitarian distribution of the redistributed wealth, would also have strengthened the authority of the central federations and hence, for other purposes, of the Foundation of Labor.

SWEDEN

Although there has been no official incomes policy in Sweden during the postwar period, the extremely high degree of union organization, amounting to more than 50 per cent of the labor force and 90 per cent of manufacturing employment, has made negotiated wages a variable of keen policy interest and has forced the parties to collective bargaining to develop alternatives which have been designed to protect their own functions and objectives and to forestall official intervention. During the sixties, however, the Swedish system, based on private control and self-discipline, came under severe strain.

ECONOMIC CONDITIONS IN THE SIXTIES

Throughout the sixties, the parties to collective bargaining operated in an environment of sustained full employment and economic growth. For 1960–1965, the unemployment rate, adjusted to U.S. definitions, was never higher than 2 per cent. Moreover, the real rate of growth was about 5 per cent per year, and the rate of increase of over-all output per man-hour was 4.3 per cent.[1] Increases in earnings including wage drift regularly exceeded the increases in labor productivity so that prices increased moderately throughout the period.

[1] OECD Economic Surveys, *Sweden* (Paris: OECD, March 1966), pp. 21, 25.

While drift had always presented a problem, it was mitigated by the ability of the Swedish economy to combine domestic price inflation with equilibrium in the balance of payments, frequently including a surplus on current account, and a high rate of growth, as noted above. An econometric analysis by Flanagan covering the period 1951–1968 reveals that the trade-off between unemployment and wage increases has been more favorable in Sweden than in any other economy in western Europe or in the United States and Canada.[2] It suggests that at an unemployment rate of 2.5 per cent increases in earnings would not exceed the trend increase in productivity. On the other hand, unemployment rose to 2.5 per cent only in the trough of the Swedish "recession" of 1958; and in 1965 the pressure of demand brought the unemployment rate down to 1.2 per cent. Hourly industrial labor costs increased 11.2 per cent, about half of which was drift, leading to a 6 per cent increase in unit labor costs (as against an average annual rise of only 2.2 per cent over the 1959–1964 period).[3] The consumer price index rose 6.2 per cent as the result of a combination of increased labor costs and an increase in indirect taxes.[4] A large deficit on current account of the balance of payments developed, leading the government to tighten further restrictive monetary and fiscal policies which had been instituted in 1963 and 1964. The deficit was gradually reduced, and in 1968 the government shifted to more expansionary policies and was aided by an increase in export demand. But gold and foreign-exchange reserves continued to fall, and when a deficit in foreign trade

[2] R. J. Flanagan, *A Study of International Differences in Phillips Curves,* unpublished Ph.D. dissertation, University of California, Berkeley, 1970.

[3] OECD Economic Surveys, *Sweden,* p. 11.

[4] *Ibid.,* p. 12.

reemerged, monetary policy was tightened and taxes raised in 1969.

A slower rise in wholesale prices due to the restrictive policies adopted in 1963 and 1964, and the generally slow increase in international prices resulted in a profit squeeze in some sectors of Swedish industry. The squeeze was viewed with particular concern in the light of Sweden's future growth potential, for a higher rate of productivity growth was required to compensate for a projected deceleration in the rate of growth in the native labor force to an annual average of 0.7 per cent in the latter half of the sixties. Yet accelerating the productivity trend required a rise in industrial fixed investment, which in turn was believed to be a function of profits. Given the additional targets in the foreign sector (restoration of current account surplus) and in public consumption, economic policy makers anticipated a problem in restraining private consumption. These economic developments focused attention on the parties responsible for wage determination and raised once again the question of the need for an official incomes policy.

PRIVATE WAGE DETERMINATION AND THE EARLY REJECTION OF INCOMES POLICY

Since the beginning of the century, both workers and employers have been represented by highly centralized organizations. Both the Confederation of Swedish Trade Unions (LO), composed of unions of craftsmen and production workers, and the Swedish Employers' Confederation (SAF) have been repositories of an exceptional degree of power over their respective affiliates; and many similar powers are held by two newer labor federations, the Central Organization of Salaried

Employees (TCO), whose affiliates represent white-collar workers, and the Swedish Confederation of Professional Associations (SACO), consisting of unions of professionals with university degrees. No firm or industry association affiliated with the SAF can take a strike, initiate a lockout, or sign a contract without the approval of the employers' federation; and the latter has the authority to order its member firms to lock out and is amply equipped with financial resources to support such struggles. With minor exceptions, the LO has analogous authority and resources; the white-collar federations, somewhat less.[5]

Ever since industrial conflict threatened to provoke national labor legislation in the 1930's, the two large central federations (LO and SAF) have been animated by a powerful drive to keep the government out of industrial relations—or to minimize the governmental role—by assuming responsibility themselves for keeping their performance socially acceptable. In the prewar period, the common task was to minimize industrial conflict, largely by creating a balance of terror, whereby either side possessed the credible threat of blowing up a sectoral conflict into almost economy-wide proportions. In the postwar period of full employment, the centralized system of collective bargaining was confronted with the problem of inflation.

The first reaction of the parties was to shoulder responsibility for wage-price behavior. The LO was motivated ideologically—first, by its desire to support the majority Social Democratic party, with which it has been extremely influential, and second, by its desire to centralize

[5] A thorough review of the history and powers of the federations is included in T. L. Johnston, *Collective Bargaining in Sweden* (London: George Allen and Unwin, Ltd., 1962).

wage determination in order to compress the industrial and occupational wage structure and equalize rates for a given occupation in accordance with its so-called "solidaristic" or egalitarian wage policy. Accordingly, the LO agreed to a voluntary wage freeze in 1949–1950, when the country experienced a balance-of-payments crisis. This attempt, however, was frustrated by local wage drift—to which Swedish labor markets are especially vulnerable because of the prevalence of piecework—and was followed by devaluation, the Korean War episode, and a wage inflation of some 20 per cent in 1951. This attempt at incomes policy was also marked by the frustration of the LO's efforts to influence the wage structure.

The episode soured the LO on incomes policy and confirmed the earlier view of its economists that the best way to minimize drift, achieve price stability, and redistribute incomes was by a combination of moderate fiscal-monetary stringency and an "active labor market policy." The latter was designed to minimize structural unemployment and wage drift caused by labor bottlenecks in conjunction with rigid wage structures. The Phillips curve was to be shifted down by such manpower policies; and the task of holding down the rate of wage increases was to remain entrusted to its traditional and natural custodian, the employer.

This, however, was the blueprint of the "LO economists," and, although it was not challenged extensively in principle, neither the Social Democratic government nor the employers' federation accepted it as policy. The former did not restrain demand sufficiently to make active labor-market policy an effective prerequisite for an approximation to full employment; and it continued for a while to exhort the unions to accept wage restraint within the limits of an announced norm. This appeal was rejected by the LO in 1952. The SAF stepped in with a proposal for a central (federation-wide) agreement, and a higher wage increase; this was accepted by the LO as a temporary measure. In 1956, however, the centralized system of wage determination was reintroduced and has been maintained to date, with the addition, in more recent years, of one of the white-collar labor federations, the TCO.

A PRIVATELY OPERATED INCOMES POLICY?

Centralized bargaining in the private sector has amounted to a privately operated incomes policy. The government is involved to some extent but only indirectly. The Minister of Finance usually offers the official view on the "room" for wage increases (based on projections prepared by the National Institute of Economic Research), and the national budget is published before the central—or "frame"—agreement is concluded by the LO and the SAF. These events may influence the parties' view of the scope for wage increases. On the other hand, the two parties prepare their own forecasts; and, as in other countries, the union forecasts have tended to be more optimistic than the official projection—and, in 1959 and 1964, they proved more accurate as well. Furthermore, the negotiators decide what development of incomes is consistent with projected economic conditions without explicit government guidelines.

More important, although the Swedish negotiations are leisurely affairs—the 1969 set ran from October to June—the over-all wage increase has usually been discussed, although not finally determined, at the outset by the heads of the two federations, in advance of the formal economic and budget discussions. The rest of the time is consumed in internal negotiations, including allocating the kitty among the different sectors, a task whose intrinsic difficulty is often compounded by the LO's adherence to an egalitarian wage policy and by the related problem of wage drift. Finally, the agreement reached by the LO and the SAF has typically preceded and set a pattern for agriculture and the public sector; and when this has not been the case, the privately run system of income determination has been threatened with dissolution.

Both sides have typically taken into consideration the wider consequences of their joint decisions. The SAF appears not only to calculate room for wage increases which are readily acceptable to the LO; its offers tend to be in the limit of its—or the economy's—calculated ability to pay, notwithstanding the existence of a squeeze on profits in recent years. It may be that this version of an employer's high-wage policy is an adaptation to the long-standing existence of a Social Democratic government; it may even represent a form of employer mediation between that government and a trade-union movement which is an extremely powerful component of the Social Democratic party in Sweden.

The LO, too, has been guided by economic and policy ramifications of its own actions. It has sought to minimize the type of governmental intervention which a highly centralized system of wage determination would tend to invite. Moreover, a centralized system is regarded as the most effective way of implementing the LO's traditional policy of wage "solidarity."

Has this sophisticated Swedish system operated to restrain wage inflation and has it yielded the type of egalitarian wage policy expected of it? Comparatively speaking, as noted above, the Swedes have fared quite well in their apparent ability to reduce inflationary pressures at relatively low levels of unemployment. But to what extent their centralized system of wage negotiations underlies this favorable trade-off relationship is unclear. One econometric analysis sought to test for such evidence by including among the explanatory variables (mainly unemployment and price changes) in its wage adjustment relationship a dummy variable. This variable was assigned a value of zero for the years 1954 and 1955 and a value of unity from 1956 on, after national bargaining had been reestablished. This coefficient was not statistically significant; so, according to this test, wage behavior was not particularly restrained by this Swedish system.[6] Nor is the profit squeeze in the late 1960's symptomatic of a successful policy of wage restraint.

Moreover, if it was indeed an LO objective to restrain general wage increases in order to create more "room" for raises for the low-paid workers, this result has not yet been appreciable. Comparisons of the relative wages of unskilled workers and of women, the two groups whose income positions the policy was particularly intended to improve, do not indicate much change, despite favorable treatment accorded in the centrally negotiated contracts.[7]

POLICY FRUSTRATION: WAGE DRIFT

The apparent inability of the centralized negotiations both to restrain the rate of increase in the general level of wages and to alter the industrial wage structure as desired are both reflected in the phenomenon of wage

[6] R. G. Bodkin, E. P. Bond, G. L. Reuber, and T. R. Robinson, *Price Stability and High Employment: The Options for Canadian Economic Policy* (Ottawa: The Economic Council for Canada, 1967), pp. 256–257.

[7] See Johnston, *op. cit.*, Chapters XVI and XVII.

COMPONENTS OF CHANGE IN HOURLY INDUSTRIAL WAGES
1963–1968
(All figures are annual per cent change.)

	1963	1964	1965	1966	1967	1968
Total hourly wage cost	8.5	8.6	11.1	9.1	9.6	6.5
Due to:						
Negotiated wage increases	3.0	2.1	3.9	4.5	4.1	3.1
Drift	3.7	4.7	5.4	4.2	4.0	3.0
Fringe benefits	1.8	1.8	1.8	0.4	1.5	0.4

SOURCE: Swedish National Institute of Economic Research; OECD Economic Surveys, *Sweden,* March 1966, p. 11, March 1969, p. 12.

drift. Drift, which is measured in Sweden as the excess of the actual over the negotiated increase in hourly earnings over the contract period, typically accounted for about half the rise in earnings (see table "Components of Change"). How much drift has been caused by employer response to specific labor shortages and how much by the successful efforts of local union groups to protect customary differentials—notwithstanding legal prohibitions against wildcat strikes—is not clear. A study by Jacobsson and Lindbeck found that the rate of wage drift as well as the rate of negotiated wage changes were responsive to the level of unemployment (which reflects the forces of demand) but not to such "ability to pay" variables as changes in productivity, profits, and prices.[8]

[8] L. Jacobsson and A. Lindbeck, "Labor Market Conditions, Wages and Inflation—Swedish Experiences 1955–67," *The Swedish Journal of Economics,* June 1969. An independent study by Anderson also shows a strong correlation between wage drift and the unemployment rate. Rolf Andersson, "Wage Drift in the Swedish Manufacturing Industry," Stockholm, 1969 (mimeographed). Reported in R. Meidner, "Active Manpower Policy and the Inflation Unemployment Dilemma," *The Swedish Journal of Economics,* September, 1969.

While the former finding is supported by other evidence, the conclusions concerning the lack of influence of other variables might be treated with some skepticism on econometric grounds.[9] Other studies indicate a significant effect of changes in prices on changes in earnings, although the latter include changes in negotiated wage rates as well as drift.[10]

To the extent that drift has been demand-determined, it might be regarded as contributing to the efficiency of the labor markets involved and thus to the profitability of the employing enterprises. On the other hand, to the extent that drift, superimposed on centrally negotiated wage increases, has contributed to general wage inflation and the squeeze on profits in the 1960's, it was regarded as unwelcome by the SAF, no less than by the LO. Moreover, Sweden has been investing heavily in her famous "active labor market" policies; and, since these are designed to cope with structural unemployment and bottleneck inflation, they are regarded as a substitute for a more flexible wage structure, with attendant inequalities.

In any event, SAF and LO have cooperated in attempts to modify their central negotiations to make them a more effective instrument in minimizing drift and in generating the kind of wage structure intended ex ante. In 1964, they

[9]The equation for negotiated wages has only seven observations, although four independent variables were normally included in the equations testing for the influence of variables other than the unemployment rate. In the drift equations, similar estimations were made on 11 observations.

[10]Cf. Flanagan, *op. cit.*, pp. 75–79, and Bodkin, *op. cit.*, pp. 256–257. The different findings of studies on quarterly and annual data concerning the influence of consumer prices may be due to the fact that the important lags (e.g., of one quarter in the earnings equation above) are not discerned in the annual data. Given the infrequency of central negotiations, the importance of price changes in the earnings equation, and the precision of the lag, it may be inferred that consumer price changes are an important determinant of drift.

devised the "wage kitty" system, whereby the increment to each industry's wage bill was to reflect the absolute difference between the mean wage in that industry and the economy-wide mean wage. In 1966, the parties concluded a three-year agreement whereby each sector could receive increases proportionate to the number of low-paid workers within it and to the deficiency of its over-all mean wage (if any); moreover, in the second and third years, industries which failed to obtain a minimum amount of wage drift in the preceding year would receive that amount as special wage-drift compensation, in an effort to prevent a deterioration in the relative wage of these industries. This was essentially an attempt to get the higher paid occupational and industrial groups to "stand still" for a redistribution of labor income in favor of the lower paid. Had it been successful, it would have achieved a classic objective of incomes policy: to induce the major wage- and price-setters to accept a given distribution of income as either desirable or inevitable. And like an effective incomes policy, the 1966 agreement would have shifted the Phillips curve downward by reducing the amount of wage increase—in this case drift—without raising the unemployment rate.[11]

Unfortunately, the 1964 agreement failed to generate the desired results—although the negotiation of such an agreement was an impressive accomplishment in its own right. In 1967 the SAF proposed tackling the problem by first estimating wage drift on the basis of drift during the preceding three-year period, taking into account deviations which might arise during the contract period as a result of predictable changes in the conditions governing

[11] The effectiveness of deflation in reducing drift as well as contractual wage increases is implied in the econometric studies relating drift functionally to the level of unemployment.

the wage drift. Next, such estimated drift, plus planned legislated changes in fringe benefits, should be deducted from the estimated scope for labor cost increases—to yield the appropriate increase in negotiated rates. This proposal, however, was rejected by the LO which objected to the implicit elimination of collective bargaining.[12]

POLICY FRUSTRATION: REVOLT BY THE UPPER SALARIAT

The architects and proponents of the Swedish system of central "frame" agreements had always regarded the persistence of wage drift as a failure of that system, but some domestic opponents regard it as a planned and integral feature. This charge has been leveled by SACO, the labor federation composed mainly of university graduates in government service and the professions. SACO claims that any restraint exhibited by LO in negotiating the frame settlements has been exercised primarily in the service of LO's solidaristic incomes policy. We have mentioned that the central settlements between LO and SAF have been intended to set a pattern for the public and agricultural sectors. But SACO points out that the higher-income salaried groups in the public sector—as well as lower-paid white-collar employees generally (many of whom are represented by unions in the TCO)—do not have as much opportunity supplement these basic wage increases with drift as do the LO's manual workers, a large percentage of whom are on piecework. Thus, while centralized bargaining has not

[12] Other LO objections to the SAF proposal included the omission of the shock effect of high wages on productivity, the possibility of deliberate bias in government forecasts and the paucity of critical data. See Stephen Anderman, "Central Wage Negotiations in Sweden; Recent Problems and Developments," *British Journal of Industrial Relations,* November, 1967, p. 334.

benefited the low-paid manual workers at the expense of their more highly paid and strategically situated colleagues, it has helped to benefit manual workers in general at the expense of (at least) the white-collar groups.

Unlike the LO, whose affiliates are industrial unions, SACO's affiliates are organized by profession and occupation and cut across industrial boundaries. Organization along these distinctive lines was intended to counteract the numerical dominance of the manual workers in private industry as well as to provide organization for higher-ranking white-collar groups in the public service. Behind the exceptionally rapid growth of SACO, which, starting in 1943, grew to include virtually all established organizations of professional workers by the mid-1950's, was a strong reaction against the egalitarian wage policy of LO and especially against the impact of inflation and a progressive tax structure on the distribution of disposable incomes. SACO claims that its average member is subject to a marginal tax rate in excess of 60 per cent and consequently has advocated a shift from direct to indirect taxation, contributory financing of social services, and the right to deduct repayments of debts incurred while studying.

But SACO's most spectacular activities occurred in collective bargaining. As indicated above, the stability of the LO-SAF mechanism has been predicated upon a pattern-setting effect on the incomes in agriculture and the public sector. Before the 1966 round of collective bargaining, however, SACO announced that the LO pattern should be applied to the disposable (after tax) incomes of its members, to compensate for their generally low ability to generate and receive wage drift. In 1966, after a bitter strike and lockout of teachers and headmasters in the schools and universities, SACO secured an average pay increase of 17 per cent, whereas the LO members in the public sector received only 5–7 per cent—a settlement which threatened the survival of the Swedish system of wage-setting.

The LO and the Social Democratic government counterattacked on the political front by emphasizing equality and by imputing on inflationary and generally antisocial role to SACO. SACO's leaders conceded that public opinion had been effectively turned against them; and, as a result of their own members' sensitivity to public opinion, SACO accepted an increase of only about 1½ per cent a year in the 1969 settlement, which amounted to a cut in real wage income of 2–3 per cent. Armed with favorable public opinion, the LO then refused to accept any settlement less than the amount groups outside the central "frame" agreement would be granted.

Moreover, the employers as well as the LO, have been opposed to SACO's objectives. For one thing, SAF is not particularly sympathetic to the white-collar unions' drive to widen or prevent the further narrowing of income differentials because it regards that move as, in the main, economically unjustified. There are relatively fewer posted vacancies for these salaried employees than for other categories; and the rapid increase in the incidence of higher education is expected further to increase the relative supply of high-level manpower.

Nevertheless, bargaining strength may run counter to long-run market forces; and the bargaining strength of some of the salaried groups, especially those in the public sector, is strong enough to threaten the Swedish wage-determining mechanism.* Thus, in the 1969 negotiations, which were extremely protracted and difficult, the

*This was written before February 1971, when a strike of 50,000 civil service workers closed the railroads, law courts, and secondary schools and resulted in emergency legislation banning strikes and lockouts.

Minister of Finance, an old trade-union leader, intervened personally in the negotiations with the State Collective Bargaining Board, which is the government's negotiating agency for its own employees and, by tradition, an autonomous agency. This departure from tradition caused strained relations with the head of the board of state mediators. Moreover, another break with established practice occurred in 1969 when a union of clerical and technical employees in private industry (SIF), which belongs to TCO, the other federation of white-collar organizations, actually settled with SAF before the LO agreement. As for SACO, its own membership was split as a result of the 1969 settlement, with the militants demanding that the organization adopt an independent bargaining policy. They argued that, as a counter to the LO's tactic of refusing to accept any frame settlement which might be exceeded by outside groups, SACO officials should formulate a set of wage demands independently of the LO's and use them as a sticking point.

POLICY FRUSTRATION: REVOLT AT THE GRASS ROOTS

Toward the end of 1969, the great European rank-and-file strike epidemic hit Sweden; and nowhere else—not even in West Germany, where unions had carried docility to an extreme—did it meet with so pained and surprised a reception. For Sweden had long enjoyed an enviable reputation for industrial peace. During the period 1955–1964, it lost an average of only 14 days per 1,000 employed; the runner-up was the Netherlands, with 53; the United Kingdom, with 294, was third in a group of the leading ten industrialized nations in the West.[13] In

[13] The Royal Commission on Trade Unions and Employer Associations, *Written Evidence of the Ministry of Labour* (London: HMSO, 1965), Appendix XVI, p. 69.

Sweden, strikes and lockouts over terms of an agreement have been illegal since 1928; but the country's record of extraordinary industrial peace is attributed primarily to the authority which the LO and the SAF have possessed with respect to their affiliates. Indeed, this authority was such that it enabled the country to couple its record of peaceful industrial relations with an equally excellent reputation for labor efficiency in the plants.

Accordingly, when the Luossavaara Kürunavaara AB (or LKAB), the largest metal mining complex in Europe and a state-owned enterprise, was shut down by a wildcat strike, the distinctive Swedish approach to industrial relations seemed to be confronted with its most serious crisis in thirty years. The challenge was underlined by the facts that the miners struck in defiance of their union leadership (a situation complicated by a struggle between Communists and the incumbent Social Democratic leadership), that one of their demands was for local negotiations with the management for new contract terms, that the strike was supported by the great mass of public opinion in the country, and that this strike was followed by other walkouts in such large enterprises as Saab, Volvo, Electrolux, Goodyear, and SAS.

Predictably, this proliferation of stoppages produced a proliferation of theories to explain the phenomenon. Of the latter, the most popular seems to be that the strikes were a manifestation of grass-roots discontent with an overly centralized institution which leaves insufficient room for individual participation in the decision-making process. This theory has the virtue of reconciling the Swedish wildcat strikes with similar strikes abroad (which also have been directed at least as much against union establishments as against employers) and with other powerful centrifugal forces which are directed against the fabric of Western social life in our time. It also suggests the late timing of the phenomenon in Sweden; if the centralized system had worked more efficiently in minimizing drift, the unrest might have come sooner.

In addition, however, it is reported that one of the principal demands was for more pay (the strikers won increases in the neighborhood of 12 per cent), that the strikers were themselves high-paid workers in highly productive and profitable lines of industry, that they complained (especially the miners) of a relative deterioration of their wages, and that they wanted their wages raised relative to the salaries of the white-collar groups (who, as we know, feel that *they* have been sacrificed on the altar of equality). This suggests that the centralized system of negotiations might have been more efficient in redistributing labor income than has been inferred from analysis of drift. It also suggests that even if such ability-to-pay factors as productivity and profitability were not too strong in the past, they might now be coming into their own as determinants of drift, although the strikes themselves and the high settlements have occurred against a background of considerable and widespread labor shortage.

Most important, however, these economic considerations suggest that discontent with the solidaristic incomes policy of the LO and the Social Democrats is found within the ranks of the LO proletariat as well as outside, as in SACO. This poses a serious threat to the LO and the SAF (whose own authority has been weakened by the settlements made by affiliated firms), for many view the principle of wage solidarity as a principal basis of the organizational solidarity of the privately operated centralized system. The threat is not necessarily fatal, however, for the system is also a product of tradition and workability; and the Swedes are long on both tradition and pragmatism. Nevertheless, if, as seems probable, the Swedes accommodate their industrial relations to the perceived need for "participation" and greater local autonomy—for example, by legalizing wildcat strikes or facilitating the development of plant-level bargaining along American lines—the impressive ingenuity of the central negotiators will face yet another stern challenge.

PROPOSAL FOR A MORE EXPLICIT GUIDEPOST POLICY

The decentralizing tendencies described in the two previous sections and emanating inside and outside the immediate domain of the central frame agreements are likely to reduce the potential efficiency in Sweden of any incomes policy of the conventional, governmentally directed variety. On the other hand, some economic developments, mainly in the later half of the sixties, apparently revived interest in the guidepost approach. Problems posed by wage drift and even by the opposition of salaried groups were regarded as supportable, because the performance of the economy continued to give satisfaction. However, the sharp rise in unit labor costs, the squeeze on profits, and the deterioration in the balance of payments in the mid-sixties induced the SAF—through its economics staff—to propose in 1967 that Sweden turn toward a more explicit form of incomes policy. The opinion that incomes policy could play a constructive role was based on the explicit assumption that the inflation problem could originate independently in the labor market which could thus be legitimately made the object of direct intervention. This assumption was regarded as plausible because since 1965 wages, unit labor costs, and domestic prices had been rising more rapidly in Sweden than in the rest of Europe, resulting in the profit squeeze in the foreign-trade sectors.

SAF proposed that future wage increases be based on a joint calculation by two economists from the SAF and one each from the LO and TCO. In the event of disagreement among these experts, the scope for increases in labor costs would be determined by a board of arbitration consisting of representatives from the employer and union sides and a jointly designated neutral. They would calculate the "scope" for the increase in labor costs, and then the probable rise in drift and legislated pensions and other fringe benefits (as noted above). The scope for increases in labor costs would be determined by jointly agreed targets for growth, productivity, investment, and the export-import sectors, and, endogenously, savings and profits.

This proposal was clearly intended to extend to SACO, for the SAF suggested that SACO join in the central bargaining on the union side. It also suggested that the State Collective Bargaining Board be invited to participate as an employer, but the invitation to a Socialist government to participate as an employer along with SAF was regarded as unrealistic. Moreover, it was obvious that the proposal excluded the government from an overt policy-making role. It has been observed that union cooperation with incomes policy frequently requires that the policy be administered by a Labor government; the SAF may reckon that, with a government sympathetic to labor so firmly entrenched in Sweden, it is preferable for it to participate actively in bipartisan decision-making which results in generous wage settlements rather than to force a Socialist government into a formal incomes policy—which, incidentally, could be counted on to include price as well as wage restraints.

Thus, although the SAF's 1967 proposal was introduced with the suggestion that the time for incomes policy might have finally come for Sweden, it relegated the government to a stand-by role with a representative on ad hoc boards of arbitration to settle disputes arising out of the interpretation of the basic SAF-LO-TCO agreements. The government was not to be represented on the boards of arbitration created in the event of deadlock over determination of the scope for labor-cost increases in the contract period ahead.

LO naturally objected to making increases in labor costs a residual and negotiated increases in negotiated wages a double residual. Its chief economist argued that causal relationships between changes in wages and in productivity ran in both directions and that using a forecast of productivity change as an instrument of policy would accord the official forecasters an incentive to bias their forecasts downward. As noted above, he argued against loss of the traditional collective-bargaining function; in particular, the assignment of priority to wage drift would induce employers to pay out more and more of their wage bill in the form of drift, leaving less and less scope for contractual wage increases. The LO reply also asserted that it was unclear how SACO and the government could participate in the negotiations.

THE AUKRUST MODEL VS. INCOMES POLICY

Although the unions were unwilling to accept the 1967 SAF proposals for a more explicit incomes policy, they did not strenuously dispute the analysis of the link between profit margins, investment, and productivity growth, although the LO maintains that their wage policies lead to productivity gains by forcing inefficient firms to close. Moreover, there was continual frustration on both sides over the persistence of domestic inflation despite efforts at restraint in negotiations. Accordingly, the next manifestation of Swedish ingenuity took the form of a joint report by the chief economists of the SAF, LO, and the TCO on the formation of wages and prices in Sweden. The report appeared as a jointly signed article in the *Swedish Journal of Economics*.[14]

In their report, the three economists found that an analysis developed earlier for Norway by Odd Aukrust was quite applicable to Swedish wage and price behavior. The crux of this model is a disaggregation of the economy into two broad sectors—an internationally competitive sector and a "sheltered" sector which produces largely for the domestic market. According to the model, wages in the competitive sector are determined by productivity growth in that sector, which generally exceeds productivity growth in the domestic sector, plus changes in international prices, which are rarely more than 1 or 2 per cent per year. These wage increases are then spread uniformly to the "sheltered" industries by "competition for labor in a full employment economy and the 'Solidarity Wage Policy'" of equal occupational rates in all industries.[15] As long as productivity increases more rapidly in the competitive international sector than in the sheltered domestic sector, domestic inflation will result, although export prices should remain stable.

The study found that productivity growth in the

[14] A summary of their final report notes at the outset that "The purpose of the 1967 SAF proposal was to systematize consideration of economic balance and growth in wage negotiations without, by doing so, increasing or formalizing the dependence of their wage policy on the economic policy of the government." See Gösta Edgren, Karl-Olof Faxén, and Clas-Erik Odhner, "Wages, Growth and the Distribution of Income," *Swedish Journal of Economics*, September 1969, p. 135.

[15] *Ibid.*, p. 142.

competitive sector, which includes half of Swedish industrial production and a fifth of total production, averaged 7.5 per cent a year between 1960 and 1967, while productivity in the sheltered sector (mostly construction and services) grew about 3.6 per cent a year. When the slight decline in public sector productivity is included, productivity growth in the sheltered sector was about 3 per cent per year during the period.[16] Moreover, the spread to the sheltered sector of wage increases geared to productivity in the competitive sector resulted in more rapid price inflation in the domestic sector (5.6 per cent per year as opposed to 1.1 per cent per year in the competitive sector during the 1960–1967 period.)[17]

Since prices are more competitively constrained in the foreign-trade sector than in the sheltered sector, wage movements in the former are more readily translated into changes in income distribution than in the latter. Operating surplus in the sheltered sector remained roughly constant at 22.8 per cent from 1960 to 1967, whereas in the competitive sector average profit margins fell from 29.5 per cent to 22.4 per cent or by 0.9 per cent per year.[18] Profit margins fell in the competitive sector because the average increase in firms' hourly labor costs was 9.4 per cent, whereas the "space for profit and wage increases" was only 8.5 per cent to 9 per cent, that is, the sum of the 7.5 per cent trend increase in productivity and the 1 to 1.5 per cent increase in world-market prices.[19]

Thus, the model explains the coexistence of domestic price inflation and a generally satisfactory balance-of-payments performance. In this situation, an incomes policy formulated along the lines of the *U.S. Guideposts,*

[16] *Ibid.*
[17] *Ibid.*
[18] *Ibid.*, p. 151.
[19] *Ibid.*, p. 146.

which required price declines in high-productivity sectors in order to achieve over-all price stability, would not work; for unlike the situation in the United States, in which many high-productivity industries appear to have discretionary pricing power, the high-productivity sectors in Sweden must take an international price as given and have no profitable reason to sell below this price. Indeed, the report is quite critical of American and British guideline policies for allegedly ignoring the strength of competitive forces in the labor market.

On the other hand, the report does not establish how much of the wage increases in the "open" sector have been necessitated by competitive pressures. The squeeze on profits in the trade sector, which occurred in Sweden, is not a necessary result of the mechanism, and may be tied to cost-push factors. It would be useful, for example, to have separate information about the sources of wage drift in the trade and domestic sectors. Moreover, the data show that the competitive sectors have accounted for a declining proportion of total output and employment. In view of the absolute and relative decline in operating profits in these sectors, it may be questioned whether a lower rate of wage increase therein would have generated much pressure on wages in the sheltered areas (which, in 1967, accounted for 70 per cent of total employment). Within the sheltered sector, the share of building in total employment rose markedly; since building is a high-wage sector, this suggests that it may have exerted upward pressures on wages elsewhere, both through market and imitative forces. (Indeed, this allegedly occurred in 1963–1964.) The Dutch objection—that the Aukrust model does not rule out sellers' inflation—is not excluded by the data and analysis presented in this report. Yet the fact that the report recommended a wage increase of 8 to 8½ per cent as the norm for the two-year period 1969–1970 indicates an impressive tribute to the strength of the SAF author's belief in his own analysis.

Despite the possible importance of these issues, the report absolves the negotiating parties of blame for inflation. The authors conclude that a governmental incomes policy is inappropriate because their analysis allegedly indicates that union wage claims have not been responsible for price increases. "The rise in prices derives from rises abroad, from the market mechanism and from strivings for equality in income."[20] They suggest that a policy which repressed wage increases in the competitive sector would only increase the demand for labor and other resources in that sector and pull up wages and prices elsewhere.

Moreover, the report, although absolving the parties of blame for inflation, offers no alternatives. It warns that a deflationary policy designed "to contend with structural price increases leads to especially undesirable effects on employment and the rate of growth. Such a policy cannot affect prices on the world market and thereby the competitive sector, nor can it affect the differences in productivity gains between the competitive and the sheltered sectors."[21] It is acknowledged that deflation could reduce both wage drift and negotiated increases in the sheltered sectors—but this is rejected because "the Solidarity Wage Policy could no longer be pursued" and because the industries thus restrained are already low-wage sectors.

LABOR-MARKET POLICY AS AN ALTERNATIVE—AND PRICE CONTROLS AS ANOTHER

The report does not seek to lighten its Strindbergian tone by plugging active labor-market policy, in which the

[20] *Ibid.*, pp. 154–155.
[21] *Ibid.*, p. 157.

Swedes have been investing so heavily. This policy in principle is designed to cope with structural unemployment and bottleneck inflation in the absence of over-all excess demand—and of incomes policy. After demand was eased in 1965, governmental appropriations for manpower and regional policies rose by 40 per cent and the number of trainees was increased from 46,000 in 1965–1966 to 85,000, or 2 per cent of the labor force, in 1968–1969. The average duration of training was over six months. These measures were popular and were credited with helping to maintain a high level of employment. Nevertheless, the very success of the program, viewed in terms of its growth, has given some economists, in both LO and SAF, some second thoughts about its economic efficiency. As long as the retraining effort was small, one could be fairly sure of securing employment for the graduates in whatever field in which they received training. But when a sizable and growing fraction of the work force is scheduled to receive training, a formidable task of forecasting demand is presented to the curriculum planners.

Moreover, the cost of raising the productivity of groups who are marginally unemployable in the absence of over-all excess demand may possibly exceed the real costs of inflation to the rest of the community. This is, of course, a judgment rather than an established cost-benefit result; but it may deter some adherents of active manpower policy from following through to its ultimate theoretical justification—the maintenance of zero or even slightly negative excess demand.

For some, these reservations have been reinforced by recent findings indicating that the labor-market programs have not succeeded in shifting the Swedish curve down. In a paper prepared for the OECD, Rudolf Meidner noted that on a Phillips curve using wage drift as the dependent variable, observations for periods in which the labor-market programs were operating on a substantial scale were above the average relation.[22] Jacobsson and Lindbeck noted a similar result for their wage-drift equation.[23] However, data for a longer time period indicate that since 1961 the annual rate of change of hourly earnings has been 1.5 per cent less than would have been predicted on the basis of the unemployment rate and consumer-price changes,[24] although this evidence does not permit the conclusion that labor-market programs were mainly responsible for the outcome.

Such evidence is in any event of limited value, because a set of active labor-market programs might be expected to exert opposite and offsetting influences on the position of a country's Phillips curve. There is some indication that, after 1965, the rate of long-duration unemployment actually rose above its predicted value. Programs to train and otherwise improve the mobility of workers should tend in themselves to reduce the average duration of unemployment. On the other hand, to the extent that other programs increase information about the labor market, unemployed wage earners might be encouraged to spend more time searching for the best jobs available; this could raise the incidence of short-duration unemployment, which would be beneficial from the viewpoint of allocative efficiency as well as individual welfare. Moreover, it has been suggested that the programs can also increase recorded unemployment by increasing labor-force participation, because one must be

[22] Rudolf Meidner, "Active Manpower Policy and the Inflation-Unemployment Dilemma," *Swedish Journal of Economics*, September, 1969, p. 167.

[23] Jacobsson and Lindbeck, *op. cit.*, p. 64.

[24] Flanagan, *op. cit.*, p. 184.

officially unemployed to qualify for most labor-market programs.[25]

For these reasons, the policy's potential for growth may detract from its potential for wage and price stability and thus as a substitute for a theoretically effective incomes policy. Certainly it did not prevent labor shortages toward the end of the decade from being accompanied by severe domestic price inflation and wage increases on the order of 10 per cent. To be sure, the inflation patterned itself somewhat on the model presented in the report: it was caused by rising import prices; and, although rising housing costs also made a contribution, productivity rose almost as rapidly as wages. But the trade deficit widened rapidly; and an increasing tendency of industrial firms, alarmed by rising costs and recent labor unrest, to increase operations abroad, contributed to a capital outflow and loss of reserves. This was a departure from the script. An even greater departure took the form of a price freeze which was introduced prior to the 1970 elections. Thus Sweden, a country without a formal policy of wage restraint, finally followed the example set by France (and later by Holland, after its wage policy had broken down) and instituted direct restraint of prices.

SUMMARY AND CONCLUSIONS

In Sweden, organized labor, management, and a Social Democratic government rejected recourse to a formal incomes policy as an anti-inflationary instrument. Instead, their long-established and highly centralized system of collective bargaining assumed an appreciable measure of responsibility for containing wage movements. Its

[25] There is some empirical support for this view. See Meidner, *op. cit.,* p. 164, and Flanagan, *op. cit.,* pp. 185–187.

effectiveness in this area has been constrained by the Federation of Labor's commitment to a more egalitarian distribution of wage income, for the higher-paid groups were able to frustrate this policy by securing additional wage increases outside the central negotiations (in the form of drift). Nevertheless, until the mid-sixties, the system served the Swedish society well. With high rates of productivity increase in the foreign-trade sector, the economy was able to combine satisfactory performance in the balance of payments, a high rate of economic growth, sustained full employment, and a politically tolerable level of price increase.

In the latter half of the sixties, however, economic performance underwent some deterioration, as the rate of increase in unit labor costs rose sharply, the balance-of-payments position weakened, and a profit squeeze threatened future growth. At the same time, the role of the bargaining system itself was threatened, first by the upper salariat—whose members' incomes were being squeezed by inflation and the operation of a progressive income-tax structure and whose ability to secure compensatory drift for themselves was extremely limited—and later by a series of wildcat strikes which were motivated in part by a revulsion against the centralized bargaining on the part of some blue-collar groups. Such developments stimulated some apparent employer interest in a governmentally operated incomes policy. On the other hand the symptoms of decentralization themselves would tend to reinforce the national skepticism about incomes policy. A more dramatic reversal of economic fortunes would seem to be required to shake the Swedes loose from their adherence to their peculiar version of laissez-faire, although a price freeze was instituted before the 1970 elections.

DENMARK

The problem which exercised the Swedes during the latter part of the 1960's had been confronted by the Danes earlier in the decade. It consisted in the increasingly limited autonomy of a centralized bargaining system which has functioned as a major determinant of the general level of costs and incomes. The Danes sought a solution in an incomes policy which featured the most comprehensive and determined attempt at "concertation" made in any of the countries surveyed in this study. Some characteristics of the Danish economy, as well as experience with alternative lines of attack, drove home the apparent need for this type of incomes policy. Some characteristics of the Danish system of collective bargaining were conducive to success. Yet some initial success was followed by failure. Some obstacles to success, like some favorable conditions, were peculiarly national in character. Others, however, were sufficiently typical to endow the Danish approach with widespread interest.

PERFORMANCE AND STRUCTURAL CHARACTERISTICS OF THE ECONOMY

The performance of the Danish economy has been characterized by a combination of relatively high degrees of inflation (averaging 2.5 per cent between 1952 and

1962), relatively high levels of unemployment, and chronic balance-of-payments difficulties. The price record began to deteriorate sharply toward the end of the fifties: between 1958 and 1967, the 5.2 per cent average annual increase in the Danish consumer price index was the highest of any country in our study.[1] Associated with price increases were increases in unit labor costs: from a ranking of eighth in a group of twelve Western countries for the period 1952 to 1958, Denmark rose to first (out of thirteen) in 1958–1965.[2]

Denmark stands out in another respect. Among those countries listed by the U.N. study as characterized by "high unemployment" (i.e., more than 2 per cent of the labor force), Denmark alone was also characterized by high sensitivity of wages to a 1 per cent change in the level of unemployment.[3] Our own wage-estimating equation for the period 1948 to 1968 also suggests wage-unemployment sensitivity. According to this equation, a rise in the rate of unemployment from 2 per cent to 3 per cent could reduce the rate of increase in hourly earnings by a third, assuming no associated change in the rate of price increase.[4]

One possible reason for the coexistence of comparatively high rates of unemployment and of inflation is that

[1] OECD, Working Party Number 4, *Demand Management, Prices and Growth* (Paris, 1969, mimeographed), p. 10.

[2] United Nations Economic Commission for Europe, *Incomes in Post-War Europe: A Study of Policies, Growth, and Distribution* (Geneva, 1967), p. 4, Chapter 3.

[3] *Ibid.*, Chapter 3, p. 14.

[4] Using annual data for the 1948–68 period we estimated

$$\dot{E} = 4.10 + \underset{(2.93)}{12.60}\, U^{-1} + \underset{(2.37)}{.347}\, \dot{P} \qquad R^2 = .56$$

in which $\dot{E}$ is the rate of change of hourly earnings in industry, U is the unemployment rate, $\dot{P}$ is the rate of change of consumer prices, and t statistics are in parentheses.

unemployment in Denmark is regarded as having a rather important structural component. Unemployment tends to be concentrated among workers in small handicrafts and among seasonal agricultural workers in Jutland. As a result of such structural imbalances among labor markets, shortages in some markets might be eliminated only by creating large pools of unemployment in others. The outcome could be an unsatisfactory compromise—more of both inflation and unemployment than the public would accept.

Moreover, this combination might well be made still more undesirable by the balance-of-payments situation. The importance of the balance of payments is obvious in an economy where exports account for roughly one-third of GNP. Moreover, the structure of Denmark's foreign trade is such that a comparatively high (by international standards) rate of inflation can oblige the authorities to force the rate of economic growth below the rate which it might have been able to achieve under less inflationary conditions. If Denmark's prices rise no more rapidly than do prices of her trading partners, the balance-of-payments position would tend to favor, rather than inhibit, growth. Demand for imports in Denmark grows more rapidly than national income—the income elasticity of import demand has been estimated by Houthakker and Magee at 1.3,[5] and this in itself is a restraint on domestic expansion. However, demand for Danish exports is still more elastic with respect to the incomes of the importing countries; the income elasticity of exports has been estimated at 1.7 by the same sources. Thus, other things being the same, the Danish economy

[5] H. Houthakker and S. Magee, "Income and Price Elasticities in World Trade," *Review of Economics and Statistics,* August 1969, p. 113.

should be able to grow up to 30 per cent more rapidly than the average rate of growth of her trading partners and still maintain equilibrium in her balance of trade. Alternatively, assuming that all economies, including Denmark's, grow at an average annual rate of 5 per cent —the actual Danish rate having averaged 5.5 per cent between 1958 and 1967—Danish exports would increase at an annual rate of 2 per cent in excess of Danish imports. If, however, the Danish export prices rise by as little as 1 per cent more rapidly than prices elsewhere this advantage would be more than wiped out. For Houthakker and Magee estimated that in response to a 1 per cent fall in price, Danish imports would rise by 1.7 per cent; and, in response to a 1 per cent rise in price, Danish exports would decline by 0.6 per cent. Thus the net effect of an all-around rate of growth of 5 per cent and a Danish differential inflation of 1 per cent would be an 8.2 per cent rise in imports and an annual rise in exports of only 8 per cent.

The classic way to restore balance, under an international regime of fixed exchange rates, is to deflate and thus reduce the rate of growth of demand for imports. This was the method to which Denmark resorted. However, apart from its inherent undesirability—aggravated by Denmark's tendency to run relatively high levels of unemployment—deflation tended to entail too much reliance on monetary restriction relative to fiscal measures. In 1965, a governmental committee called attention to an interesting asymmetry: when deflation was called for, parliament was reluctant to raise taxes or restrict government expenditures, so that the burden fell on the National Bank and monetary policy; but when reflation became feasible, parliament was willing enough to reduce taxes or spend more, so that the bank and the interest rates were left high and dry.[6] This ratcheting of interest rates was believed to inhibit the role of investment in upswings, to the detriment of industrialization of the economy and of growth in the share of exports—for which demand appeared so strong.

THE INFLUENCE OF THE BARGAINING SYSTEM; DRIFT, ESCALATION, AND INTERACTION

But if lack of coordination between official policy centers made it difficult to handle the problem of inflation by monetary and fiscal measures, lack of coordination between public policy-making in general and private decision-taking in the labor sector was, in the opinion of the committee referred to above, a major cause of the trouble in the first place. It was felt that, as an authoritative commentator later put it, "the increasing power of the parties in the labour market made them really set the pace for money incomes in the whole country, or wage incomes at any rate."[7]

In fact, the Danish system has been characterized by sufficient scope and centralization to endow the labor side with significant bargaining power. At the same time, some features have made the system responsive to pressures from below, which makes for a high degree of utilization of labor's potential bargaining power.

The Danish work force is highly organized; collective-bargaining coverage of wage earners is almost complete in manufacturing, construction, and transportation; and the organization of salaried employees, especially in the public sector, has been growing rapidly.[8] More than half

[6] *On Incomes Policy: Papers and Proceedings in Honour of Erik Lundberg* (Stockholm: The Industrial Council for Social and Economic Studies, 1969), pp. 41–42 (comment by Carl Iversen).

[7] *Ibid.*

[8] W. Fellner, *et al., The Problem of Rising Prices* (Paris: The Organization for European Economic Co-operation, 1961), pp. 285–286.

the membership is divided almost equally between one giant general workers' union of unskilled workers (the DASF) and a large number (71) of craft unions for skilled workers. However, the great majority of these unions (in addition to the large Federation of Metal Workers and Engineers) are affiliated with the Danish Federation of Trade Unions (LO) which bargains for the labor side in central negotiations with the Danish Employers' Confederation (DAF). The latter, through its affiliates, represents about half of industrial production and controls, like its Swedish counterpart, the formal bargaining and the lockout activities of member firms. Moreover, smaller employer federations in other sectors normally follow its lead in collective bargaining.

Although craft organization has resulted in a multiplicity of separate collective agreements, all have uniform expiration dates and directly reflect the main changes negotiated by the two central federations. The authority of the central organizations over their respective affiliates – which on the labor side has been traditionally resisted by the big general workers' union – tends to be buttressed by two public arbitration institutions. Disputes over the interpretation of existing agreements may be submitted to a Permanent Court of Arbitration, but only by the federations. And impasses in major negotiations are subject to a process of *ad hoc* mediation by state arbitrators, who are empowered to declare a cooling-off period of fourteen days. These mediators may publicize their own recommendations; and if they are ignored by the parties, it is customary for parliament to pass legislation enacting them. But before that ultimate step is taken, the mediator can submit his proposal to a referendum of the members of the two organizations. In practice, however, the mediator will refuse to make recommendations if he feels that he cannot secure acceptance by both parties lest he impair his future usefulness;[9] and a prime object of the issuance of third-party recommendations is to enable the negotiators to pass the buck and thus to sell difficult settlements to their respective sides. Since parliament has been understandably reluctant to engage in legislative wage-setting, there is considerable pressure to generate and ratify such negotiated recommendations.

While this unique system of mediation has tended to strengthen the hand of the central labor negotiators, the referendum feature obviously transmits rank-and-file pressure upward. One source of such pressure is found in conflicts of interest between lower-paid and higher-paid workers. These conflicts cannot readily be resolved or compromised at the level of the affiliated national unions, since Danish unionists are organized along occupational lines, instead of in industrial unions which would more frequently include both low-paid and high-paid workers in the same organization. As a result, the LO has been obliged to contend with these issues directly; partly in order to retain the allegiance of the big union of unskilled workers (the DASF), it has adopted a "solidaristic" or egalitarian wage policy calling for uniform absolute increases (including cost-of-living supplements) for low-paid workers.[10]

However, one reason why the central system of negotiations has proved to be a fairly viable institution in Denmark is that the higher-paid workers and their unions have been able to circumvent the solidaristic policy. This has been accomplished through compensatory movements in wage drift whereby skilled workers have been able to reestablish differentials in earnings at the plant

[9] Walter Galenson, *The Danish System of Labor Relations* (Cambridge, Mass.: Harvard University Press, 1952), p. 124.

[10] Fellner, *op. cit.*, p. 287.

level.[11] Both the tendency to seek compression of the wage structure through central bargaining and the frustration of this tendency through local wage-setting are familiar phenomena in Scandinavia. In Denmark, however, both phenomena have been intensified by the structural peculiarities of the union movement. Not only has the solidaristic wage policy, a by-product of the Socialist ethic, been reinforced by the pressure exerted on the LO by the general workers' union, but the ability of high-paid groups to get their own back has been enhanced by "the general lack of mobility in the Danish labour market stemming from institutional factors such as the craft basis of union organisations and the elaborate apprenticeship system."[12] Moreover, two additional factors have facilitated local wage increases through individual bargaining. In the first place, about 40 per cent of the workers in manufacturing and construction are on piecework. In the second place, the rates established for about half of the time workers in central negotiations are only minima; it is provided that premiums above these minima are to be established in accordance with individual levels of experience and skill. Finally, while these premiums were supposed to be established only by individual bargaining, in practice, groups of skilled employees would jointly negotiate their premiums.

As a result, wage drift has been particularly troublesome to economic policymakers in Denmark. To begin with, it has accounted for a major proportion of increases in total earnings. Of the 5.4 per cent average annual rate of increase in hourly earnings between April 1953 and April 1960, 2.3 per cent was accounted for by wage drift. During the 1960's, drift generally accounted for

[11] *Ibid.*, pp. 300–305.
[12] *Ibid.*, p. 303.

roughly a third of increased earnings, and for one-half thereafter.[13]

Moreover—and unlike the behavior observed for other countries—much Danish drift appears to have been independent of general economic conditions and therefore not readily susceptible to restraint by deflationary action. This phenomenon was first noted by the OECD study in the early sixties and has more recently been confirmed by a U.N. study which noted:

> In Belgium and Denmark the short-term relationship hardly exists, although there . . . is a suggestion that the long-term downward trend in unemployment is associated with some increase in the amount of drift.[14]

The problem of drift in Denmark may therefore have a considerably greater cost-push element to it and hence be of greater policy concern than is true in Sweden and other countries. The estimating equation set out in footnote 4 above, on the other hand, shows an apparent sensitivity of changes in over-all earnings to short swings in unemployment, which is somewhat puzzling in view of the fact that the centrally negotiated biennial wage increases themselves show little variation. It may be that part of drift is indeed sensitive to changes in the over-all level of demand. The influence of the insensitive components of wage increase, including the remainder of drift, would then be reflected in the positive constant term which suggests that, even at indefinitely large levels of unemployment and in the absence of changes in the cost of living, hourly earnings could have been expected to rise at an average steady rate of 4 per cent a year during the

[13] *Ibid.*, p. 293; OECD Economic Surveys, *Denmark.* February 1967, p. 10; April, 1968, p. 10; June, 1969, p. 12.

[14] U.N. Economic Commission for Europe, *op. cit.*, Chapter 3, p. 22.

period 1948 to 1968. In any event, the most compelling evidence is that furnished by the persistence of high rates of drift during years when unemployment exceeded 5 per cent of the work force.

Another distinctive feature of the Danish system of collective bargaining is the inclusion of an automatic escalator clause, whereby a flat cost-of-living wage supplement is awarded for a minimum absolute rise in an official cost-of-living index, which originally included changes in tax payments as well as various types of transfer payments. Introduced in 1918 after a period of wartime inflation, indexation was abandoned at the insistence of the unions in 1930, in order to avert wage cuts. It was reinstated in 1945, but the employers were able subsequently to resist union attempts to incorporate the cost-of-living supplements into the basic wage. The employers' objective was to maximize the potential downward flexibility of total compensation as much as possible.[15] In one respect they have succeeded, since, as we have noted, most of the increases in earnings have been increases in both the cost-of-living increments and in drift. The question is: To what extent have the employers paid for this hedge against deflation with inflationary wage movements during the long postwar expansion?

Although a system of wage indexation which provides for semiannual cost-of-living adjustments is, on its face, potentially an inflationary institution, it has been argued that, in fact, the price has not been too great. One reason given is that, were it not for semiannual cost-of-living adjustments, the LO would have followed common practice elsewhere by insisting on one-year contracts instead of accepting contracts of two and three years'

[15] Galenson, *op. cit.*, p. 152.

duration.[16] It is also relevant to recall that the cost-of-living supplements have been paid out on the basis of a flat amount for a rise of a specified number of points in the index. This was done at the insistence of the union side to further the objective of wage equalization.[17] However, since money wages have risen more rapidly than prices in the postwar period, the system has yielded decreasing compensation, on a percentage basis, for price increases. The relatively small coefficient of the price-change variable in our own equation (footnote 4), which suggests that barely more than a third of any price increase is translated into a wage increase is not inconsistent with such attrition. On the other hand, since the system of uniform absolute compensation might be intended to equalize labor incomes, it is likely to generate offsetting wage drift for higher-income workers. Since drift lags behind centrally administered wage changes (which, moreover, tended to be concentrated in the first year of the contract period before 1963), the full effect of a rise in consumer prices on money earnings would be distributed over time. As a result, the price coefficient in an equation like ours would not capture the full impact; some of the remainder might show up in the constant term. This type of linkage between prices and wages tends to limit the effectiveness of such intended correctives to maladjustments in the balance of payments as deflationary measures or currency devaluation, for it makes for inflation short of full employment and tends to deflect resources away from exports and investment in the process.

Of more immediate concern to policy makers in the mid-fifties, however, was a more indirect effect of the

[16] Fellner, *op. cit.*, p. 297.
[17] Galenson, *op. cit.*, p. 151.

Danish bargaining system—a "drift" of nonwage incomes in response to wage movements, and the associated danger of potential leap-frogging. The ability of a collective bargaining system to exert leverage on the general level of money wages and of incomes in general is a function of the extent of collective bargaining coverage, for the smaller the uncovered area, the less likely it is to absorb the impact of negotiated increases elsewhere through reduction in its own relative income. Thus the tendency of both salaries and per capita incomes in general to move in line with industrial wages in Denmark in the fifties[18] might have reflected, to some extent, the high degree of organization in the labor sector. Moreover, this type of extended drift allegedly fed back into the central wage bargaining itself. According to Carl Iversen,

> The usual order of timing was that the wages should be negotiated before 1st March, and the others successively during the summer, and consequently the wage earners would be reluctant to accept a moderate increase until they knew what consequences it would have for the other groups, because they would fear that these groups would on that basis claim to get not only compensation but overcompensation.[19]

THE SOCIAL CONTRACT

In view of the unpromising structural characteristics of the economy's labor markets and foreign trade and of the apparent inflationary potential of the collective-bargaining system, it is not surprising that policy makers began to give serious consideration to incomes policy. The investigating committee had made recommendations along this line in 1956, but it was not until 1962—or after two

[18] Fellner, *op. cit.,* p. 293.
[19] *On Incomes Policy,* p. 43.

successive small external deficits in 1960 and 1961 and a more serious one the following year—that parliament was moved to pass legislation. The approach taken in 1962 reflected the policy makers' emphasis on workability. They were determined to avoid the *Guidepost* approach of the Kennedy administration because they regarded the guideposts (especially on the price side) as nonoperational. An earlier British approach, although an improvement insofar as it provided for a review mechanism in the form of a Council of Prices, Productivity, and Incomes, was also regarded as unsatisfactory because the unions declined representation. Insistence that the policy be made operational reflected Danish belief in the inflationary potential of sequential income determination, as described above; a sequence of settlements involving the collective-bargaining sector, the civil service, and agriculture in 1961 received a good share of blame for the ensuing inflation and deficit on foreign account.[20]

The Danish solution was to pass a law (in itself a departure from American and early British practice) establishing an Economic Council with some twenty members representing unions, employers, the civil service, agriculture, and the handicrafts. In addition the Ministries of Finance and of Economics and the Danish National Bank were also represented. Finally, provision was made for a three-man Board of Chairmen, which has been composed of academic economists.

> Now the philosophy was that this group, consisting of people who were responsible for the various parts of economic policy, and usually meeting only when they were sitting on each side of the table negotiating with one another as opponents, should also come together regularly in another setting, sitting, so to speak, round the table where they could confidentially discuss

[20] Erik Hoffmeyer, "Incomes Policy in Denmark: Recent Developments," *British Journal of Industrial Relations,* November 1964, p. 352.

one another's viewpoints, and learn from one another. Of course, it couldn't do away with the conflict of interests, but still it might make the whole discussion a little more intelligent.[21]

The chairmen, however, were granted considerable autonomy. They were supposed to hold their own meetings (as well as convene the entire council at least twice a year), and they were empowered to issue policy statements, independently of the rest of the council. The board proceeded to take the lead at the outset. Confronted with a wage explosion of 15 per cent, with the recent introduction of new tax measures which were only temporary, and with the onset of negotiations in the wage sector, over government salaries, and over agricultural subsidies and market prices, the board made two major recommendations. The first was that all three sets of bargains be concluded together—the so-called "simultaneous solution." The second recommendation was that, in view of the large deficit in the balance of payments, all money incomes be frozen.[22] These recommendations were accepted in principle by the various groups represented on the council, including the government; but the employers and unions couldn't agree on how to implement them. Mediation proved unavailing, but the coalition government enacted into law a set of provisions based on the recommendations of the Board of Chairmen—who thus discharged the task of furnishing recommendations to parliament which the mediators had found it impossible to perform under conditions of deadlock. The 1963 legislative package contained the following major provisions:[23]

A temporary freeze on contractual incomes for two years, except for the inclusion of previously agreed minor

[21] *On Incomes Policy*, p. 42.
[22] *Ibid.*, p. 43.
[23] Hoffmeyer, *op. cit.*, pp. 352–354.

adjustments and a general increase of 2 ½ per cent in the second year.

A kitty of 1.25 per cent of the total wage bill to be distributed among the lowest-paid groups, which was supposed to minimize so-called "imitative drift." Salary increases for the lowest-paid civil servants and increases in social security pensions and sickness insurance payments.

Retention of the cost-of-living escalator, but without reflecting the impact of tax increases.

No increase in agricultural subsidies.

Regulation of prices and profit margins, which: (a) required advance notification to the Monopolies Board of price increases as well as increases in costs of purchasing, production, or distribution; (b) denied wage increases in excess of those permissible under the wage legislation as a basis for price increases; and (c) provided that absolute profit margins not exceed the levels prevailing at the time of passage of the price legislation (February 1963).

A freeze on dividend payments and directors' fees.

IMPLEMENTATION IN PRINCIPLE

Although these restraints were legislated for only a two-year period, it was hoped that a new type of policy, however modest, might emerge on a more voluntary and permanent basis. And although great importance was attached to the simultaneous determination of money incomes, it was felt that the critical determinant of the policy's over-all effectiveness lay in the capacity to restrain the central collective bargaining. Still more specifically, the major restraining influence had to come from the union side of the bargaining table. A premium was placed on maximizing the degree of employment, partly perhaps because it was a policy objective to lessen the country's dependence on agricultural exports and this could most rapidly be achieved by maintaining a currency which was undervalued with respect to industrial output. Thus incomes policy was supposed to help administer over-all excess demand. Under these conditions, management cannot be expected to hold down prices of wages; the Danes do not credit their employers' association – notwithstanding its considerable control over the collective bargaining activities of its affiliates – with as much power or inclination to restrain price behavior as their German counterparts are credited with. Thus wages had to be restrained directly and the unions had to hold the reins.

Moreover, the unions were credited with sufficient power to impose wage restraint, given sufficient inclination to do so. This did not necessarily mean that the unions were to "blame" for wage inflation; on the contrary, the modest portions of past increases in earnings accounted for by the central negotiations almost suggested that the LO might have had the capability of acting as a sort of counterweight had it chosen to do so. Therefore the task of policy was to convince the unions that if they wanted full employment, they had to act as a counterweight against inflationary tendencies of whatever origin. And for the unions to accept this role, they had to be persuaded that the other economic interests in the community could not profit from their restraint. This was the subordinate task which the price, profit, and dividend policies were assigned. (Such policies were assigned the same task in Britain before the 1967 devaluation.)

PERFORMANCE AND ENVIRONMENT

The new incomes policy was credited with a high degree of effectiveness in 1963 and 1964. Many observers regarded the outcome as almost too good to be true, and unfortunately it was. For the policy operated in the presence of a number of special conditions which contributed to the effectiveness of an incomes policy or operated independently as stabilizing influences. In the first place, there was a serious balance-of-payments problem—the classic stimulus to the promulgation and support of incomes policy. Secondly, the policy was launched shortly after demand management had taken a deflationary turn—in response to the same set of problems which had triggered the incomes policy itself. Thus it was observed that "this overall solution was very successful, particularly during the first year. The counterpart of that, however, was that growth was halted, so that the national product increased by only 1.5 per cent, whereas it had usually gone up by 3–4.5 per cent."[24] Thirdly, although the Economic Council itself was legislated as a permanent institution, the specific wage and price restraints took the form of a temporary, one-year freeze. Fourth, the governing coalition which pushed the legislation through included the Social Democratic party, with which the LO has always maintained a close working relationship. And finally, the government made a direct contribution to the simultaneous solution by actively restraining wages in the public sector.

In retrospect it appears that an unfavorable prognosis for the policy's effectiveness in the absence of these special conditions would have been justified. In addition to reducing the rate of increase in negotiated rates, the legislated restraints had the effect of eliminating the "front-loading" which had characterized some earlier two-year agreements. Thus, whereas hourly earnings had risen by 12 per cent in 1961 and then 9.4 per cent in

[24] *On Incomes Policy,* p. 43.

1962, the rates of increase in 1963 and 1964 dropped to 8.7 per cent and 7.7 per cent, respectively.[25] On a cumulative basis, these figures represented a decline in the rate of increase of over a quarter from the first two-year contract period to the second. But this deceleration was associated with a sharp rise in unemployment between 1962 and 1963 (from 3 to 4.2 per cent and, for the skilled male building workers, from 1.8 per cent to 4.4 per cent).[26] The recorded deceleration in wages—which, in any event, was not as dramatic as the emergency measures might have led a devotee of the British freeze of 1966–1967 to expect—presumably reflected this marked decline in economic activity. On the basis of our estimating equation the wage increases recorded in 1963 and 1964 were indeed lower than expected on the basis of prevailing levels of unemployment and prevailing rates of price increase, but not outstandingly lower. In 1963, the divergence (which was half a percentage point) was appreciable by postwar standards; but the 1964 overprediction (of two tenths of a percentage point) was quite small.[27] The relevant values (which were drawn from different data sources from that referred to in footnote 26 above) are:

Year	Rate of Insured Unemployment	Percentage Change in Consumer Prices	Percentage Change in Hourly Earnings	
			Recorded	Estimated
1963	4.3	5.2	8.7	8.9
1964	2.9	4.0	9.1	9.6

Wage increases might have been further restrained by the operation of the price and profit controls. Our wage-estimating equation cannot take such indirect influence

[25] *Incomes in Post-War Europe,* Chapter 3, p. 32.
[26] OECD Economic Surveys, *Denmark,* June, 1969, p. 46.
[27] See footnote 4.

into account; however, the price increases which occurred in 1963 and 1964 – 5.2 per cent and 4.0 per cent respectively – were not minimal.

If the policy was not very good when times were good for it, how good could it be when times got bad for it – that is, after the controls were revoked by administrative decree (in October 1963) and after unemployment fell? In fact, unemployment fell sharply (from 4.2 per cent in 1963 to 2.4 per cent in 1964 and 2.0 per cent in 1965); the rate of wage increase jumped up to 11.5 per cent in 1964; and for the next two-year period, the rate of wage increase was just about what one might have predicted on the basis of prevailing rates of unemployment and price change.

THE PUBLIC SECTOR AND THE SIMULTANEOUS SOLUTION

In part the Danish partial freeze resembled the British "pay pause" of 1961–1962, since both relied heavily and, in the end, unsuccessfully on using the public sector as a pausemaker. Under the terms of a new Civil Servants Act which had been passed after the negotiation of the 1958 central wage agreement, salaries in the public sector had been linked to wages in the private sector.[28] The simultaneous solution of 1963, however, restricted increases in civil-service salaries to low-paid groups; and, although wages in the private sector were of course to be restrained as well, the civil servants were squeezed especially hard. Following campaign promises, the government awarded large pay increases to its employees in 1965. It sought to rectify the inequities which had occurred during the

[28] Fellner, *op. cit.*, p. 310.

freeze early enough to clear the decks for the central negotiations. The theory seemed to be that LO and its adherents would then have no cause to fear that their acceptance of a 3 per cent norm for money incomes would be undermined by the subsequent granting of a larger increase to the government sector. This move, however, failed; the private sector determined to catch up on the civil servants' catch-up increase. What this episode seems to have demonstrated is the wisdom of the earlier Danish practice—and the Dutch policy as well—of assigning priority to the maintenance of "comparability" between labor incomes in public and in private employment and the unwisdom—at least as far as longer-run policy is concerned—of attempting to slow down an inflationary chariot by a significantly one-sided tug on the reins.

The experience of 1963–1965 also revealed implicitly the distinction to be drawn between the "simultaneous solution" and consensus on the distribution of income, and the limitations as well as the importance of each to the effectiveness of the other. Consensus alone need not suffice; under already inflationary conditions each party to a consensus might feel obliged to leap-frog over his neighbor in order to maintain or regain his agreed-on share of the income. On the other hand, mere elimination of sequential income determination would not ensure consensus. The keen interest which the Danish experiment with simultaneous determination aroused in Swedish circles was stimulated by the threat posed to the stability of the Swedish system of collective bargaining by SACO, the union of professional people and university graduates. But the Danish experience with the government sector doubtless reminds the Swedes that the trade-off between redistributive policies not based on consensus (and even if effected through the political process) and wage-price stability can be fairly steep.

BETWEEN DRIFT AND NORM: THE RESIDUAL ROLE OF COLLECTIVE BARGAINING

The Danish experience also suggests that, for collective bargaining to play an effective role in wage-price stabilization, the need for consensus on the distribution of wage income within the bargaining sector can be no less compelling than the need for a wider distributional consensus, involving the bargaining sector itself as well as all others which are represented by powerful claimant groups. The existence of uniform expiration dates has made possible centralized bargaining and the uniformity of substantive provisions in more than three thousand separate contracts; but this absence of sequential wage determination did not eliminate drift. The policy makers of 1963 did make a serious effort to minimize drift. The special provision for the low-paid reflected an attempt to secure agreement by other groups that the low-paid were to receive differential treatment. Moreover claims for drift payments by sizable groups of workers in large establishments, which usually found their way to the central bargaining table, were "systematically rejected in accordance with the spirit of the act."[29] Yet the policy makers were realistic. Although the special kitty was to be parceled out among the lowest-paid groups by the parties—subject to arbitration in the event of disagreement—"it proved extremely difficult . . . to establish sensible criteria for such a distribution."[30]

[29] Hoffmeyer, *op. cit.*, p. 353.
[30] *Ibid.*

And although every effort was made to eliminate group drift, individual drift payments could not be prohibited since many collective agreements set only minimum base rates. The upshot was that the controls of 1963 did not result in the elimination of drift. Indeed, given the reduction in the centrally negotiated increases for the two-year period, drift occupied a somewhat higher proportion (about one-half) of the total increase in earnings than previously. The total drift—amounting to a 5.6 per cent rise in hourly earnings—was equally divided between the two years, despite the sharp drop in unemployment in 1964. But these results probably reflected a more even temporal distribution in the centrally negotiated rate increases; and it certainly reflected the relatively low sensitivity to demand conditions traditionally exhibited by Danish drift.

But if the drift problem was not, predictably, aggravated by improvement in the economic climate, it was certainly not neutralized by the more liberal and, hopefully, long-run phase of incomes policy which emerged in that climate. With the crisis and the negotiations for 1965–1967 approaching, the Economic Council's Board of Chairmen tried their hand at "a very simple guide for the rise in income for the whole population which would be compatible with a fairly stable price level."[31] Allowing for the probable per capita increase in GNP and the probable improvement in terms of trade, the chairmen set a 3 per cent annual increase in per capita income as "the frame within which money income had to be restricted." The bargainers accepted the guidepost but threw away the frame: " . . . they had eaten the whole cake, so to speak, by the general collective bar-

[31] *On Incomes Policy,* p. 44.

gaining, and not left anything over for wage drift."[32] The result was that the wage drift which in fact occurred also touched off the cost-of-living escalator. So, whereas the negotiated rate increases were 3 per cent in both years, the rise in hourly earnings came to 11.7 per cent and 9.1 per cent, respectively.

The next time around, the chairmen tried a different approach, which included publishing two guideposts—a larger one for per capita income and a smaller one for the central negotiators. After calculating a permissible increase in per capita income of 6 per cent for the year beginning March 1967 and also for the year thereafter (on the basis of estimated improvements in productivity and in the terms of trade), they assigned 2.5 per cent of this to drift—"as much as we had in the best three years in the 1950's," according to Iversen, and a bit less than in 1963 and 1964—and another 1.5 per cent to an automatic cost-of-living supplement estimated on the basis of some continued price inflation (which at the time was in excess of 6 per cent a year). This left 2 per cent for the central negotiators, who were thus cast in the role of residual claimants. By treating drift as exogenously determined, the chairmen were in effect treating the distribution of wage income in its most controversial dimension as beyond the reach of incomes policy. And their somewhat similar allowance for cost-of-living increases was consistent with the view that the broader functional distribution of income had to be taken for granted: in fact, "we asked ourselves if the trade unions could squeeze profits, and we said that previous experience has shown that the probability was very small."[33] Prior allowance for the rise in the cost of living, al-

[32] *Ibid.*
[33] *Ibid.*

though realistic, also seemed to indicate that relatively little reliance could be place on direct price control; in fact, it had earlier been felt that the price freeze of 1963 would result in distortions of the price structure and should therefore be only temporary.[34] That left collective bargaining as the only recognized target for incomes policy. The bargainers, however, were apparently deaf to this call to greatness; they picked up the 2 per cent general increase but then helped themselves to an additional increase of 2.5 per cent to compensate for a two-hour reduction in the work week. Drift and price inflation did, of course, materialize; hourly earnings rose 9.6 per cent in 1967 and, after devaluation, about 13 per cent in 1968.

The outcome of the 1966 negotiations was another facet of Danish experience which held interest for the Swedes. Swedish employer representatives tentatively floated the residual model as a trial balloon in 1967, and Swedish union representatives promptly objected, primarily on the grounds that it robbed collective bargaining and, to a considerable extent, trade unions of their *raison d'être.* Their reaction—like the response of their Danish colleagues—is certainly plausible. But were the Danish chairmen completely unrealistic in 1966? In the light of the relatively modest portions of past wage increases which had been accounted for by the central negotiations, it would not have been unreasonable (as suggested earlier) to regard them as a potentially stabilizing element. Yet it does not follow that this potential could be more efficiently realized under a formal incomes policy aimed at holding all per capita increments to income within stated limits. For the publication of such a norm virtually ensured that the LO

[34] Hoffmeyer, *op. cit.,* p. 353.

negotiations would have to take "the whole cake themselves"; and this, in turn, would imply assuring a residual role to drift, rather than central bargaining. (This task, as we know, had been beyond the capacity of the central bargainers even under conditions of slack demand and unemployment. A combination of full employment and wage policy after 1963 resulted in a *de facto* alliance of shop stewards and plant managers applying irresistible pressure for group drift.)

The problem was intensified by the publication of norms in the neighborhood of 3 per cent three times running and spanning a period of six consecutive years (1965–1971). The Danes thus unwittingly dramatized the dilemma posed for collective bargaining by a wage policy based on a norm determined predominantly by foreseeable movements in over-all productivity. The unions reacted in two ways. In the first place, union spokesmen (among others) began to oppose the publication of norms. (This implicitly rejected the American model of the coercive *Guidepost,* but, as we have seen, the Danes had earlier rejected this approach as nonoperational.) The second reaction of the unions was to press for income statistics in apparently ever-increasing detail and apparently with two purposes in mind. They wanted detailed data on occupational incomes to support particular claims on the basis of comparability; and by demanding data on the personal distribution of income and even assets they demonstrated lack of acceptance of the existing distribution of the national income. Neither strategy speaks well for incomes policy.

POLITICS AND INCOMES POLICY

We listed the inclusion of the Social Democratic party in the government as conducive to success of the 1963 policy. In the light of experience elsewhere, this is hardly a startling claim; in Denmark, however, it is supported by some rather interesting evidence. In the first place, while the 1963 legislative package was passed in response to a general economic crisis, it was opposed by the opposition in parliament and by employers, who feared that, in the end, prices and dividends would be more effectively restrained than wages. Therefore the LO's support of the measure, which was regarded as essential to the stability of a government led by the Social Democrats, was politically crucial, since the measure passed by a very narrow margin.[35]

The second piece of evidence was provided during the election campaign which followed as a result of the Danish devaluation (of 7.9 per cent) in late 1967. Devaluation had been preceded, first by rapidly rising wages, prices, and deficits on current account, and next by the introduction of a value-added tax which contributed to a rise in both prices and unemployment. The deflationary conditions were conducive to the effectiveness of the devaluation (although they had been insufficient to obviate its necessity), but the forthcoming cost-of-living increase in wages was feared as a perversely neutralizing influence. So the government proposed a suspension for one year (and, possibly, eventual elimination) of the wage escalator as part of a revived incomes policy; and the LO obliged its political ally by accepting. The left-wing Socialists, however, opposed the idea, and so did the conservative parties in the opposition.

The final evidence came after the election when, having won the election, the center-right coalition tried to interest the unions in essentially the same proposition which their opponents had previously raised. They also held out a carrot, in the form of a partial freeze on prices

[35] *Ibid.*, p. 352.

and profit margins in 1968, under which price rises could reflect rises in centrally negotiated wage rates but not drift or cost-of-living increases. And they waved a stick: the unions were warned that, if they refused to modify the terms of the 1967 agreements, the government would have to deflate. The LO pointed out that, only a few months earlier, they had acted responsibly while the parties now in the government had not; and they turned down the government's proposal—presumably on the theory that turn about is fair play. Whereupon the government did increase taxation to restrain consumption.

The government also went ahead with price controls, notwithstanding its failure to secure union cooperation in restraining labor costs. It extended until November 1968 a freeze on profit margins which had been imposed after the devaluation, introduced a partial price freeze on some services, and made retail-price-maintenance arrangements subject to control by the Monopoly Control Board.[36] To the extent that direct restraint on prices and profits could either substitute for or indirectly induce wage restraint, this experience under a conservative government could count as evidence against our contention that incomes policy is likely to be more effective when parties with close ties to trade unions are in power. For, if wage-restraint policies are more readily supported by unions when Social Democrats are in office, price restraints can be imposed by conservative governments. But the object of Danish price-profits policy has been more to reassure the unions that wage restraint would not result in an adverse redistribution of income in favor of profits; it was not intended to squeeze employers into greater resistance to union wage demands. There was talk of promulgating a new price freeze be-

[36] OECD Economic Surveys, *Denmark,* April, 1968, p. 17.

fore the beginning of the 1969 negotiations in an effort to moderate the outcome; but there was little disposition to face the prospect of a general strike if the unions decided to throw down the gauntlet.

These negotiations were conducted against a background of high unemployment and were included after intervention by the state mediator. But his proposal, which was accepted by a narrow majority vote,[37] called for another basic increase of 3 per cent a year, thus making no allowance for drift and price increases. With the resumption of boom conditions, the annual rate of increase in hourly earnings rose to 12 per cent in 1969 and the deficit on foreign account reached a record high. Once again (in 1970), the government resorted to a partial freeze on service prices. This time, however, it made no attempt to stop the operation of the cost-of-living escalator. Instead, it announced its intention of covering wage increments generated by that escalator with subsidies to employers.[38]

SUMMARY AND PROSPECTS

The Danes, like the Swedes, have a system of collective bargaining which is highly centralized and, on the union side, committed to economic egalitarianism. As such it may have acted as both a stimulus and an offset to wage drift; and it may have also stimulated destabilizing competitive reactions by other centers of income determination in the economy (notably the public sector).

In Denmark, however, balance-of-payment problems have been more acute throughout the postwar period. Other structural characteristics of the Danish economy

[37] U.S. Bureau of Labor Statistics, *Labor Developments Abroad,* July, 1969, p. 4–5.

[38] *The Economist,* August 15, 1970, p. 72.

have made for an unfortunate combination of relatively high levels of unemployment (especially in the fifties) and rates of inflation. The Danes seem to have been less willing than their Scandinavian neighbors to embrace the Aukrust model of "imported inflation" which, granted its explanatory virtues, has served as a pacifier for those who might otherwise have been tempted to cry aloud for incomes policy. There is strong opinion that Danish inflation has a substantial home-grown component, frequently originating in the "sheltered" construction sector and thus capable, through diffusion, of causing damage to the economy's export-import position.

In any event, the Danes, unlike the Swedes (after the immediate postwar years), did turn to formal incomes policy in an effort to cope with some of their problems. Notably included among the latter was the problem of competitive and sequential income determination, involving the private sector (under central bargaining), the government, and agriculture. Their approach in 1962–1963 to a "simultaneous solution" was legislated and included the creation of an Economic Council, composed of representatives from the major interest groups as well as official policy centers and presided over by a partly autonomous Board of Chairmen. The original policy package also included a temporary and partial freeze on wages, prices, profit margins, and dividend payments. Exceptional payments were granted to low-paid groups in order to minimize "imitative" drift in the private sector and to make the "average" and higher-paid groups of public employees bear a heavy share of the over-all burden of restraint. Tax increases were omitted from the consumer price index in order to eliminate perverse wage escalation.

These emergency measures imposed some restraint on

wages in 1963 and 1964. However, the effectiveness of this policy was underwritten by the existence of facilitating conditions: a balance of payments crisis; demand deflation; the "freeze" nature of the policy itself (which had the effect of putting the awkward question of income distribution on ice); tight restraint on government salaries; and a governing coalition which included the Social Democrats, the unions' political associates. With the disappearance of these conditions, incomes policy had to depend on the council, on the wage norms which its chairmen issued, and later (in 1968 and 1970) on the imposition of price freezes by a conservative government. The publication of a productivity-based and relatively invariant norm might have had the perverse effect of making the Danish Federation of Labor less willing to adapt to drift and cost-of-living escalation by restraining the centrally negotiated portion of wage increases.

In the future, Danish policy makers are likely to concentrate more on labor-market policies as a way of easing the trade-off between unemployment and inflation. It is hoped that such policies might reduce wage pressures originating in construction, which is a high-wage sector, and ultimately facilitate the redeployment of labor from construction to exports and import substitutes without an abortive and therefore inflationary attempt to narrow wage differentials. Moreover, to the extent that labor-market policies could reduce drift generally by eliminating labor bottlenecks it could remove a major obstacle to the success of incomes policy.

For the Danes are not yet ready to give up on incomes policy. The promise of "concertation," Danish-style, has not been fulfilled; the union leaders were unwilling—and in any event could not afford—to accept existing distributions of income, either within or reaching beyond the bargaining sector. Nevertheless incomes policy has been credited with some pedagogical effectiveness. Before 1962, when the Economic Council was established, the unions reacted hostilely to any suggestion that wages were an important economic variable, in trade-off terms. Now this notion is no longer disputed; and this – when one considers the considerable political and policy-making power of the unions – is an appreciable social gain. Indeed, their increased economic sophistication might have made Danish unionists – many of whom represent rigorously circumscribed craft jurisdictions – more receptive to active labor-market policies than they would have been at the end of the fifties, especially in view of the heightened embarrassment to which central negotiators are subjected by drift when they must also live with a norm for incomes.

FRANCE

France, in an apparent inversion of the design of postwar incomes policies observed in other countries in this study, has relied almost exclusively on price control as a method of indirect wage control as well as a direct anti-inflationary device. Attempts to specify and administer wage guidelines have not been notably successful, although official interest in structural reform of wage-setting institutions, which would facilitate more direct control over wages, persists. The French approach to incomes policy is understandable given the rather peculiar nature of the country's labor movement and its system of industrial organization and also in the light of some aspects of wage-and-price behavior, which in turn reflect these organizational peculiarities. Recourse to direct controls is also understandable in view of the rather prominent role assigned to national planning in the development of French economic policy.

MARKET INSTITUTIONS AND THE NATURE OF FRENCH INFLATION

Trade unionism in France has long been characterized by organizational weakness and doctrinal division. At most 30 per cent—more realistically 20 per cent—of the nonfarm labor force is organized; and dues-paying membership accounts for no more than 5 to 10 per cent.

Trade unionists are organized into four nationwide federations. The largest is the General Confederation of Trade Unions (CGT) which has been Communist-dominated since the end of World War II and, for ideological reasons—rooted in the exceptionally stubborn syndicalist traditions of the French working class[1]—has opposed collective bargaining in principle, if not always in practice. The other three federations are the French Democratic Labor Confederation (CFDT), which began as the left wing of the Catholic political party, the Socialist-oriented Force Ouvrière (FO), which was formed by an anti-Communist secession from the CGT and whose main strength is in the civil service; and the small but growing Conféderation Génerale des Cadres (CGC), a pressure group of white-collar and civil-service employees. These groups have cooperated on occasion, mainly in strike activity, but their interrelationship has been dominated by ideological conflict and by competition. This has tended to minimize dues income and direct bargaining strength.

These characteristics, however, do not imply that organized labor in France has no muscle. Its political influence, while nebulous, has been significant. Even under the Gaullist regime it was accorded status as an interest group; thus it has been formally represented on the Conseil supérieur du Plan, although its representatives have not been noticeably effective. More importantly, the unions have been able to generate numerous flash strikes and other brief but widespread stoppages; on such occasions dues-paying membership is a poor indicator of worker support. But this type of bargaining

[1] Everett M. Kassalow, *Trade Unions and Industrial Relations: An International Comparison* (New York: Random House, 1969), pp. 100–116.

power is exercised primarily against the government and the general public, rather than against employers at the level of industry or plant. It stands in contrast to the American system. Under the latter, pressure on "third parties" is discouraged by legal constraint as well as union inclination; while the party of the second part, the employer, is legally obliged to bargain in good faith with (but only with) a duly certified representative of the majority of his employees in a well-defined bargaining unit. In France, indeed, a law was passed at the end of World War II which provided for collective bargaining in a series of industrial, regional, and plant-level "conventions." These agreements were given the status of statutory minimum rates; and the Minister of Labor was empowered to "extend" the terms of such contracts to nonsignatory firms. But no obligation to bargain was laid on the employers, and the latter tenaciously resisted union attempts to introduce collective bargaining, especially at the plant or firm level. This generally rigid employer attitude, combined with—and doubtless contributing to—a worker movement structurally and temperamentally ill-suited to conventional collective bargaining, relegated the legal framework to the status of an economically dead letter. The conventional rates became "minima supplemented by various premium systems and special rates determined at the enterprise level"[2]—and determined unilaterally at that level.

Employers are organized into associations, partly for the purpose of bargaining at industry or regional levels. But the conventional rates thus established are generally pitched to the pay levels prevailing in the lowest-paying

[2] Economic Commission for Europe, *Incomes in Post-War Europe: A Study of Policies, Growth and Distribution* (Geneva: United Nations, 1967), Chapter 4, p. 22.

enterprises. This, of course, is not an uncommon characteristic of industry-wide bargaining. But, although union pressure has been effectively exerted at either plant- or industry-wide level in other countries, in France direct visible evidence of such pressure is for the most part absent.

In view of the unique institutional influences to which the labor markets in France have been exposed, what role can be assigned to French unions in accounting for movements of money wages and prices? A very minor one, in the opinion of many academic and foreign observers. For example, an OECD committee of independent experts, studying inflation in the fifties, concluded:

> Among the industrial countries, France presents a special case where very strong excess demand, even though it lasted for a relatively short period, was clearly the major factor in the rise of prices, and where wages chase up behind prices in a more or less typical price-wage spiral. Under these circumstances, it is hard to say whether an independent role can be attributed to collective bargaining. As regards the private sector, the limited scope of large-scale bargaining and the lack of unity in the trade union movement suggest that this is not likely to have been the case on a significant scale.[3]

The quotation refers to the fact that inflation came to France in a series of short spurts—in the early 50's, in 1956–1958, in 1961–1962, and after the "events of May" 1968—rather than as a gradual and continual phenomenon which might have been more suggestive of a steady push upward on wages.

On the other hand, another school of thought, which seems to have prevailed among the planning experts, has viewed French inflation as partly a cost-push phenomenon, although of a rather subtle variety. According to

[3] W. Fellner, *et. al., The Problem of Rising Prices* (Paris: OECD, 1961), p. 46.

this view, the inflation of the early 1960's was the outcome of a process of intersectoral competition. In part, this competition arose in response to shortages of skilled workers and is thus understandable as a conventional competitive phenomenon. But the quasi-cost-push theory goes on to stress that the competing sectors are oligopolistically organized with considerable discretionary control over pricing. Given the strong French tradition of state-protected cartelization, reinforced by "mixed enterprise" (state and private joint ownership or control) in some of the most advanced industrial sectors, it is not difficult to appreciate why such a theory should have gained currency.

Moreover, analysis of French wage movements hints at behavioral peculiarities for which a naïve demand-pull hypothesis would provide no better an explanation than would a naïve cost-push hypothesis. For, while the rate of increase in money wages has reflected the level of excess demand (as measured by the level of unemployment) or its rate of increase (as measured by the rate of change in the difference between the number of registered unemployed and the number of unfilled vacancies), it has clearly been affected by other factors as well.[4] One

[4]The observations in the text are our inferences from two econometric studies: R. G. Bodkin, E. P. Bond, G. L. Reuber, and T. R. Robinson, *Price Stability and High Employment,* Special Study No. 5, prepared for the Economic Council of Canada (Ottawa: Queen's Printer, 1967), pp. 243–248; and Michael Evans, *An Econometric Model of the French Economy* (Paris: OECD, March 1969), pp. 30–34.

In developing an econometric model of the French economy from annual data from 1951–1965, Evans estimated the following equation:

$$\dot{W} = .057 + \underset{(.220)}{1.293}\,\dot{P}_{-\frac{1}{2}} - \underset{(.123)}{.536}\,(\dot{U - V}) - \underset{(.145)}{.241}\,\dot{W}_{-1}$$

$$R^2 = .812 \qquad d = 1.75$$

in which $\dot{W}$ is the rate of change of average *yearly* earnings of all wage and salary workers, $\dot{P}_{-\frac{1}{2}}$ is the rate of change of consumer prices, study found a significant negative relationship between the rate of increase in money wages and the reciprocal of a time trend, which, it held, "implies that there has been an upward shift over time in the wage adjustment relationship for France, but that this upward shift has occurred at a diminishing rate."[5] The time trend may be a proxy for an increase in cost-push forces. This might mean that the chosen instruments of the French union movement—the flash strike and, on occasion, the quasi-general stoppage—might have reinforced its general sociopolitical influence to some economic effect. The

---

lagged one-half year. $(\dot{U-V})$ is the *rate of change* of the difference between the number of registered unemployed and the number of unfilled vacancies and the standard errors are in parenthesis. Evans reports that a version of the equation using the *level* of (U−V)—i.e., the standard (theoretical) Phillips curve version—performed less well and that the coefficient on (U−V) was not statistically significant.

However, few of the features of Evans' wage determination equation are evident in the findings of the other study, although there are differences in the data and time period used. Using quarterly data on *hourly* earnings in industry and some services and the unemployment *rate* for the period 1954 I – 1965 IV, the Canadian economists estimated the following equations (t statistics in parentheses):

$$\dot{W} = 11.07 + \underset{(2.87)}{13.56}\, U^{-2} - \underset{(3.25)}{31.31}\, t^{-1} - \underset{(3.55)}{.56}\, DUM{\cdot}t - \underset{(2.75)}{.40}\, \dot{W}_{-4}$$
$$R^2 = .387 \qquad d = .42$$

$$\dot{W} = 10.94 + \underset{(2.85)}{13.60}\, U^{-2} - \underset{(3.15)}{30.57}\, t^{-1} - \underset{(3.38)}{2.60}\, DUM - \underset{(2.67)}{.395}\, \dot{W}_{-4}$$
$$R^2 = .375 \qquad d = .42$$

in which t^{-1} is the reciprocal of a time trend, DUM is a dummy variable taking the value zero for observations prior to the fourth quarter of 1963 and unity thereafter and DUM·t increases linearly from 1963 IV.

These authors report that the rate of change of the Consumer Price Index was *not* a statistically significant determinant of wage increases during this period. They suggest that there may be deficiencies in the construction of the French Consumer Price Index, but it seems equally likely that, given the use of quarterly data and Evans' strong results using lagged annual data, the lag structure may have been improperly specified in the Canadian experiments.

[5] Bodkin, *op. cit.*, p. 244.

"explosion" which occurred in May–June 1968, when money wages were raised by more than 10 per cent (13–14 per cent for the entire year) might have given evidence of the unions' ability to exert third-party pushfulness, for it occurred in the face of excess capacity and historically high unemployment. (The number of unemployed had increased by about 50 per cent from mid-1967 to mid-1968, when it reached 2.6 per cent. The push took the form of a three-week general strike affecting more than ten million of the nation's fifteen million wage and salary workers, and it culminated in the *Protocole de Grenelle,* a centralized agreement between the union federations, the government, and the employers' association.)

Evans' study (see footnote 4) indicated that wage movements in France have been highly responsive to prior changes in consumer prices, after allowing for changes in the degree of excess demand. Moreover, the coefficient of the price-change variable in this study is significantly greater than unity, suggesting the existence of some mechanism which was able to overcompensate wage earners for increases in the cost of living. This of course does not deny that both wage and price increases reflected the proximate influence of excess demand, because unemployment in France has invariably been low by American standards. But such evidence might suggest that the operation of French labor institutions, combined with the organization of the product markets, forced the authorities into somewhat more inflationary policies than would otherwise have been required, in order to maintain desired rates of employment and growth.

Moreover, the apparent responsiveness of wages to price increases might be regarded as confirming the French authorities in their recourse to an incomes policy which emphasized direct pressure on prices. As noted in footnote 4, the Canadian study did not find price movements to be a significant source of wage increases. However, this study did find indirect evidence (in the form of statistically significant dummy variables) that an incomes policy introduced in 1963 tended to retard wage increases. Since this policy (which was also associated with deflation) relied on strong price controls as well as on attempts to hold back pay increases in the public sectors, the significant dummy variables might have captured some unspecified price effect on wage movements.

INCOMES POLICY THROUGH PRICE CONTROL

Whatever its motivation or justification, the French government throughout much of the postwar period has acted as if control of market prices would induce wage restraint in the face of excess demand and would also limit the discretionary pricing power of large enterprises.

The legal basis for price control in France dates back to early World War II legislation, and although most available price controls are now exercised only in emergency conditions, existing legislation enables the government to return to a system of control at any time. This happened repeatedly in the fifties (in 1952, 1954, 1956, and 1957). In 1958 the old system of price controls (which apparently led to considerable relative price distortion in some sectors) was dismantled, but it was reactivated with a price freeze in 1963. This price freeze accompanied a "guiding light" on wages and salaries and deflationary measures adopted in the aftermath of a "wage explosion" in 1961–1962.

The French have developed a greater variety of price-control devices than any of our sample countries. The exact mechanism of control has varied between sectors.[6] Maximum prices are frequently enforced for several basic agricultural products and foodstuffs, several services, and a few industrial products. Prices are determined from cost data which firms are legally required to provide. The government also sets prices in the nationalized coal, gas, and electricity industry, although subsidies are granted to those sectors if it appears that a price increase would have a significant effect on the general price level.

For several other products the French have developed the innovation of the constructed price increase, in which the producer calculates (and may have to justify) his price according to rules set down by the administration. A more widespread practice, however, is the advance notification of price increases, which are assumed to be approved unless explicitly questioned.

In an effort to relax the price controls instituted in September 1963, the government announced a form of "contractual" price freedom for employers who were willing to sign long-term *contrats de programme* (planning contracts) with the government for the duration of the 1966–1970 Fifth Economic Development Plan. These contracts have included sectoral guidelines for price increases and for the allocation of productivity gains between wages, dividends, investment, and developmental research; but they permitted industries freedom in price determination if the latter agreed to a compulsory review procedure.[7] Advance notification of price increases continued in sectors of high inflationary

[6] For a complete catalogue of techniques which have been used since 1939, see OECD, *Policies for Prices, Profits and Other Non-Wage Incomes* (Paris: OECD, 1964), pp. 60–62.

[7] OECD Economic Surveys, *France* (Paris: OECD, May 1967), p. 27.

potential; and industries which did not choose to sign planning contracts remained subject to the 1963 controls. By the autumn of 1968 these agreements covered 80 per cent of industry; in addition, ten contracts were in existence in the trade and service sectors.[8]

Unlike its response to the wage explosion of 1961–1962, the government did not freeze prices after the wage explosion of 1968. Since the disruptions of mid-1968 occurred at a time of considerable slack in the economy, the government decided to continue an ongoing policy of reflation in the hope that the increases in wages and salaries would be absorbed by rising output and productivity. Moreover, profits had been depressed, and it was feared that a price freeze would drive many small marginal entrepreneurs (always a politically potent group in France) out of business. Accordingly, it continued to rely on the *contrats de programme* in the private sector and on more direct price restraint in the public sector. But it allowed the prices of bread and autos to rise at once, and this action raised the fear of union reaction. Together with the appearance of a deficit on current account, this apprehension helped to generate a large deficit on capital account and a currency crisis in November 1968.

The government then switched to a deflationary policy, including credit restriction, to protect the franc. Moreover, in the meeting of March 1969 (which had been promised in the Grenelle settlement of 1968), it resisted union demands for wage increases totaling about 8 per cent; these included full compensation for increases in the cost of living since the Grenelle *Protocole*. The government offered only 4 per cent in compensation for price increases in the first quarter of 1969, and it faced down threats of another general strike. These moves, however, failed to forestall devaluation, which occurred

[8] *Ibid.*, (April 1969), p. 30.

in August 1969. After devaluation, the government adopted a policy reminiscent of its "stabilization program" of 1963: deflation plus a temporary price freeze, followed by a resumption of price restraint through an intensified administration of *contrats de programme*. And the government announced that no further global "confrontations" with labor would be held.

It is nevertheless doubtful whether France's characteristically one-sided approach to incomes policy will prove to have survived the May 1968 events and the 1969 devaluation without modification. This is not because price policy seemed to be exceptionally ineffective during that period. Between April 1968 and April 1969 (the twelve-month period beginning with the wage explosion) consumer prices rose only 6.2 per cent although the increase in money wages was 17 per cent. In the second half of 1969 (during which the devaluation occurred), consumer prices rose only 2.7 per cent; and in the twelve months following September 1968, real wages rose only 1.3 per cent, the lowest rate for the comparable period in six years.[9] But the experience of the late 1960's underscored the economic and political limitations of price policy in France. Evans' results imply that successful restraint of prices could lead to an absolute reduction in real wages. But even if it merely—but noticeably—tended to reduce the rate of advance in real wages, it could provoke union reaction—which in France has meant political confrontation with the government. On the other hand, to the extent that price control is unable to restrain wages sufficiently for the policy purpose at hand (e.g., balance-of-payments equilibrium), deflation is required; and this stunts economic growth. To combine a rigorously expansionist monetary-fiscal policy with a

[9]The Economist Intelligence Unit, *Quarterly Economic Reviews: France,* 1969, No. 1, p. 10; No. 2, p. 7; No. 4, pp. 7–8.

satisfactory balance-of-payments performance—something which France had been unable to do in 1968 (and which a Conservative government in Britain had failed to do in 1964)—would not a more direct and effective policy of wage restraint seem to be indicated?

INCOMES POLICY AND NATIONAL ECONOMIC PLANNING

In fact, the potential importance of incomes policy in achieving targeted rates of economic growth had for some time been keenly appreciated in the *Commissariat der Plan.* While the economy moved out of the phase of postwar reconstruction, it became increasingly subject to international pressures, both economic and political. More recently, the planning process itself, which during the fifties had been tightly controlled by an elite corps of civil servants, was opened up to greater parliamentary control over the "grandes lignes" of the plan, including the desired distribution of realized incremental income and the distribution of potential income between output and leisure.[10] As the planners became subject (not necessarily against their personal inclinations) to increasing market and political constraints, incomes policy commended itself to them both as a means of maintaining mutual consistency among output and distributional targets *(cohérence)* and as a partial substitute for other instruments which were becoming less accessible to the authorities.

Thus, while it had been possible to keep public investment on target during the deflation of 1958–1959, long-term growth targets had to be sacrificed in the "stabilization program" of 1963–1964. This helped to induce the planners, then led by Commissaire Général Pierre Massé,

[10] Andrew Shonfield, *Modern Capitalism* (New York and London: Oxford University Press, 1965), pp. 125–145.

to seek a long-term incomes policy. It was hoped that incomes policy—as the expression of a consensus among the various economic interests—would help the planners to specify guidelines governing the distribution of the gains of projected growth; and it was hoped that, through consensus, inflation could be minimized and the growth targets could thus be reached. Incomes policy was also viewed as a replacement for public control over credit, which had proved to be an effective disciplinary instrument when firms threatened to exceed their investment quotas under the plan—or to go in for unauthorized price increases. This instrument was being eroded by growth in self-financing and, together with other types of control, by France's entry into the Common Market. Moreover, increased self-financing and a larger share of profits were set as targets by the planners; the share of wages and salaries had increased substantially in the early 1960's and the planners wished to arrest this trend. At the same time they wished to achieve a relative rise in the incomes of the poorest sections in the population.

Accordingly, Massé convened a conference on incomes policy consisting of nine separate meetings attended by planning officials and representatives of employers' associations, trade-union federations, and farm organizations during the period October 1963 to January 1964. The objective was to achieve *concertation* (mutual agreement) by these groups on the distribution of personal income within the context of medium-term planning. But the conference failed to produce agreement on this basic issue; it was called "a dialogue of mutes."

The main employers' federation (the *Patronat*) objected to planning and forecasting, fearing encroachment on entrepreneurial initiative, although a smaller group of "young employers" approved. The union federations were opposed on grounds of their own ideology;

and they were angered over the recent passage of legislation restricting the right to strike. The largest federation, the CGT, held that planning under a Gaullist regime could not alter the essential nature of the class struggle. The smaller FO was also opposed; its strength was concentrated in the public sector, and the government was moving to determine wages in the civil service directly and to "recommend" increases for public corporations and to outlaw strikes. The CFDT, however, which was developing a new militancy and later threatened to outflank the CGT on the left, expressed interest in the objective of "social justice," or differential gains for the low-paid. But the CFDT representatives insisted, as a *quid pro quo,* that the legally established works committees of employees – whose authority precluded negotiations and grievance handling – be furnished specific information on the investment, employment, and wage policies of firms. They also insisted that entrepreneurial discretion be replaced by joint determination of real earnings and of industrial and occupational wage differentials (as indeed the law had envisaged). Finally, the labor representatives complained that the statistical basis of forecasting in the areas of wages and other incomes was extremely poor; and two unions suggested the establishment of an independent Institute of Statistics to improve information in this area.[11]

Despite the failure of Massé's conference, the Fifth Economic Development Plan included the following specific income guidelines for achieving stability of unit labor costs:[12]

[11] See especially J. E. S. Hayward, "Interest Groups and Incomes Policy in France," *British Journal of Industrial Relations,* July 1966, pp. 165–200.

[12] U.S. Bureau of Labor Statistics, *Labor Developments Abroad,* September 1967, p. 14.

Income Group	Maximum annual percentage rate of growth of income
Farmers	4.8
Entrepreneurs	3.3
Upgraded workers	3.3
Others	2.8

The plan also called for industrial price reductions and for an increase in self-financing.

The government hoped that these "indicative norms" would find acceptance in public opinion and thereby constrain the negotiating parties. It also hoped that the generation of data on productivity and distribution of income originating in particular industries or enterprises would work to the same end. The creation of an agency generating such data, known as the Center for the Study of Incomes and Costs (CERC), was nearly all that Massé had been able to salvage from the wreckage of his conference. He had been obliged to abandon his proposal for a more ambitious College for the Study and Evaluation of Incomes (CEAR), which would have been empowered to calculate and publicly criticize excessive increases in wages and other incomes. Instead, taking at face value the unions' objections to the paucity and quality of statistical information required for incomes policy, the government set up the new center, which may not attempt publicly to influence the setting of wages and prices. On the other hand, it may produce reports on the request of the government or the Economic and Social Council (on which the major economic interests are represented); and it has in fact been producing technical studies, including the development of some ideas of Massé and others on the measurement of total factor productivity at the enterprise level and the annual allocation of this surplus to wages, profits, and price changes.

But the government did not entrust the fate of its indicative norms solely to moral suasion, social pressure, and quantitative enlightenment. It also deployed more direct and coercive measures: controls over prices and over wages and salaries in the public sector. As noted above, price controls were later relaxed (in 1966) with the introduction of the *contrats de programme*. The latter were made available to enterprises as an alternative to statutory control over their prices, and also as a condition of receiving favorable consideration with respect to the allocation of outside capital.

On the wage front the authorities were less successful. In 1964, the government adopted a new three-stage procedure for determining the wages of public employees. A group of committees headed by a single high state official was to determine the recent rate of increase of earnings in the various nationalized sectors, after which the government would make its proposal for a global wage increase which it deemed consistent with the objectives of the plan. The unions were to be left with the task of negotiating with management the distribution of the global increase among the various categories of workers. In the spring of 1966, however, the unions found fault with the government's global offer. The unions argued that in view of price increases during the previous year (2.8 per cent) the real wage increase implicit in the offer was less than the (3 per cent) increase "promised" in the plan, but the latter had not in fact been obtained at that time. There ensued a series of strikes and also a period of formal cooperation between the CGT and the CFDT on nonideological issues.[13] In a sense these developments

[13] The cooperation was really a sign of the weakness of the individual organizations. During much of the period, the strike was only sustained by rotating the work stoppages between unions for a few hours at a time.

set the stage for the events of 1968, although they were dominated and obscured by the student uprising and other elements of social unrest.

The indicative norms for the growth of incomes were thoroughly shattered by the general strike of May and June 1968. The *Protocole de Grenelle,* the agreement which ended the workers' strike, provided for wage increases of 4.5 to 5 per cent on June 1, and another 2.5 to 3 per cent on October 1. The OECD estimates of the actual wage increases between January and October 1968 indicate that the greatest increases occurred in sectors where government pressure to restrain wages had been greatest in the preceding years. Although the general manufacturing increase was between 11 and 13 per cent, increases in central government and nationalized industries were 15–15.5 per cent and increases in local government amounted to 19 per cent.

Thus, while the planning contracts might have had some direct effect in restraining prices, this clearly wasn't sufficient to hold down the rate of increase in money wages. In fact, real wages rose 10 per cent between October 1967 and October 1968, in comparison to a rise of 2.8 per cent in the preceding twelve months.[14] Thus, in the absence of an effective restraint on wages, restraint on prices resulted in an excessive rise in real wages, given the planning targets.

CONCERTATION THROUGH PARTICIPATION?

Although the planners failed to get *concertation* in one swoop in 1963–1964, they did not give up the attempt to secure voluntary restraint in the interest of *cohérence.* Instead, they switched to a lower-keyed, informal, and

[14] OECD Economic Surveys, *France* (Paris: OECD, April 1969), p. 9.

gradual approach. In its statistical work, the Center for the Study of Incomes and Costs has maintained close working relationships with members of union research staffs. Its object has been gradually to build up union confidence in the quality and objectivity of CERC's statistics and econometric analysis so that both sides might learn to "speak the same language."

Nevertheless, limits are imposed on the effectiveness of this strategy by the nature of the relationship between the labor movement and the government in France. There is, first, the political conflict between relatively venerable ideologies—the Old Left ideology of the Communist-led CGT and the precapitalist nationalist ideology personified, at least until recently, by General de Gaulle. Second, in the trade-off between growth and consumption, union and government interests are invariably opposed to some degree, although the extent of divergence is affected by the political coloration on each side. Partly because the French have institutionalized planning, French unionists have explicitly posed the issue as growth versus labor income. They publicly criticized the Pompidou government for embedding too high a target growth rate—6 per cent—in the sixth plan, because they feared that resources will be diverted to investment from social-assistance programs.[15] (An announced reduction in social-assistance benefits, combined with a rise in contributions, had contributed to trade-union militancy in May-June 1968.)

Confronted with these obstacles to *concertation,* the authorities started to experiment cautiously with a different approach to industrial relations and to incomes policy. Under de Gaulle the French began to talk up *participation;* and, like "automobile," this linguistic

[15] *New York Times,* April 6, 1970.

innovation has gained international currency. *Participation* is a blanket term, covering a wide variety of practices which range from profit-sharing, employee stock ownership, and the processing of plant grievances by workers' councils to "codetermination," or the seating of union representatives on company boards (in Germany and the Netherlands), and a voice in the selection and compensation of plant managers (in Yugoslavia). To an American, the concept might invoke memories of corporate paternalism (including employee-representation plans) in the twenties or simply bring to mind contemporary plant grievance machinery. But to a Gaullist *participation* was welcome as yet another anti-Communist alternative to Anglo-American institutions, a socioeconomic *force de frappe*.

Originally, the French appeared to emphasize financial rather than representational schemes. An ordinance of 1967 spells out the rights of employees to conclude agreements establishing profit-sharing (or productivity-sharing) arrangements whereby special payments to employees would be withheld in personal accounts for five years. Such funds are invested in the enterprise itself. Moreover, participating firms are granted certain tax allowances.

More ambitious experiments were instituted in 1969 and 1970. One of these consisted of an offer of shares to employees in the nationalized Régie Renault. Another was the encouragement of bilateral, long-term (two years) agreements in the public sector. These so-called *contrats de progrès social* link wage increases to cost-of-living increases and both general and sectoral increases in productivity. They also establish dispute-settlement tribunals, in exchange for a no-strike agreement.[16] And

[16] U.S. Department of Labor, *Labor Developments Abroad*, July 1970, p. 14.

consistent with the wage yardsticks in the *contrats de progrès* (if somewhat remote from their participatory innovations) was a revision of the national minimum wage. This not only eliminated the former ten-month lag of changes in the minimum wage behind movements in the cost-of-living index; it also provides for linkages of the minimum wage to the economy-wide rate of growth.[17] Finally, under government sponsorship and initiative, the unions and the central employers' association signed a master agreement calling for a changeover (by 1975) to *mensualisation,* whereby hourly paid workers would henceforth be paid, like white-collar employees, on a monthly basis, with a thirteenth month of pay and with comparable seniority-graded benefits, sick pay, and pensions.[18]

Some of these innovations will burden labor costs considerably. *Mensualisation* alone, which would be phased in over a number of years, could ultimately raise labor costs by as much as 25 per cent in some enterprises; thus far it has already increased them by about 9 per cent on the average. On the other hand, settlements in the private sector ran at an annual rate of about 11 per cent in 1969.[19] It appears that the French authorities tried to divert cost increases which would have occurred in any event into new channels which would hopefully facilitate economic growth and also minimize their inflationary impact. The *contrats de progrès* are obviously aimed in these directions; they are intended to enlist worker cooperation in raising productivity and were in part inspired by the impetus which British incomes policy placed behind productivity bargaining.

[17] *Ibid.,* p. 15.

[18] *New York Times,* May 2, 1970.

[19] OECD Economic Surveys, *France* (Paris: OECD, March 1970), p. 28.

Profit-sharing in the form of what has elsewhere been termed "investment wages" would help the planners in their attempt to increase self-financing and thus release resources for investment in plant and equipment. *Mensualisation,* by increasing the relative attractiveness of blue-collar occupations, is supposed to help ease shortages caused by a drain of blue-collar labor into white-collar jobs. Finally, the changes in the procedures and criteria employed in the revision of the minimum wage were consistent with the planners' objective of coupling a higher rate of investment and growth with a redistribution of income in favor of the poor.

The prospects of some of these ambitious changes are uncertain. As far as profit-sharing is concerned, coverage under an optional scheme, begun in 1959, reached only 1.5 per cent of the work force in 1965. The Renault scheme was attacked by the CGT on the ground that, by permitting the resale of shares distributed to employees, it would lead to denationalization of public enterprise. It was later amended by restricting such sales to a special company fund; moreover, no more than 25 per cent of the shares will be made available for employee distribution. Nevertheless, surveys have shown little worker enthusiasm for this form of "people's capitalism" in the past; income from stock ownership would represent too small a fraction of total worker income to arouse great enthusiasm.

In assessing the future of the more procedural aspects of worker participation, one should not ignore the postwar history of French workers' councils. Since the end of World War II firms with fifty or more employees have been required by law to establish a joint plant committee or Works Council. Employee members are elected from lists of names submitted by the unions. One indication of the failure of the *participation* idea so far is that by official estimates less than 50 per cent of the potential councils were active.[20] Moreover, the work of the active councils was only obliquely related to raising productivity. Although the councils can be consulted by the employer on any issue, in practice they have been accorded responsibility only for the management of various welfare activities of the firm. There is a widespread feeling that employers have shifted most of their social service activities to the councils as a way of keeping them out of the financial and economic activities of the firm.

However, "joint consultation" in Great Britain has proved equally disappointing; and in both countries, the plant committees' activities did not include collective bargaining. But just as productivity bargaining in Britain is intended to link decisions affecting productivity with the joint determination of pay, so the French *contrats de progrès* are intended to serve the same function. The CGT has, predictably, opposed these contracts as an exercise in class collaboration. Early in 1970 it held a referendum among gas and electricity workers, who voted to reject such a contract at the time. On the other hand, *mensualisation* has been a popular issue among unionists and workers generally; and the unions did sign a long-term contract of progress with Renault. It will be recalled that, during the abortive incomes conference of 1963–1964, the more venturesome CFDT had expressed interest in *concertation* if it included active union participation at the plant and enterprise level; and it is interesting that the two non-Communist federations did sign agreements in nationalized industries (electricity and gas, railways, and coal mines) in 1970. The Pompidou "new

[20] A. Sturmthal, *Workers Councils* (Cambridge: Harvard University Press, 1964), p. 44; Chapter II.

deal" caught the CGT in one of its weak spots—continued adherence to an ideology which has been or is in the process of being relegated to largely ceremonial status by Socialist and even Communist organizations elsewhere in Europe.

The new initiative has also touched another sensitive nerve of French unionism: structural weakness at the plant level. Here, fears that *participation* in the form of contracts of progress might result in old-fashioned company unionism might not prove unfounded, since the French unions (like unions in the rest of Europe) have not sunk deep roots at the plant level. But the authorities deny that their interest is to weaken French unionism. On the contrary, they argue, only with strong unions at the plant level can sufficient progress be made in terms of industrial efficiency—and wage-price stability. Economic planners are logicians; French economic planners are Gallic logicians; and logic dictates that organizations must be powerful before they can be responsive.

CONCLUSION

In France, efforts to restrain prices and wages have consisted primarily of price controls, rather than wage guidelines. The persistence of ideological opposition to collective bargaining, both within the labor movement and among employers, the weakness of union organization within product and labor markets, and the apparent dominance of demand influences on wage movements help to explain the relative lack of extensive experimentation with wage policy. At the same time, highly oligopolistic organization of important product markets and the existence of an important sector of nationalized industry have made recourse to price control understandable.

On the other hand, some econometric evidence suggests that wage movements in France have not been free of "cost-push" influences, an inference which is reinforced by the occurrence of a wage "explosion" in May-June 1968, which occurred against a background of rising and high unemployment and excess capacity. Such evidence is consistent with the view that the type of pressure traditionally generated by French unions—emanating from widespread nuisance strikes and an extra-parliamentary political presence—justified some efforts which were made during the sixties to develop a viable policy of wage restraint. In fact, such an incomes policy was viewed as essential to the avoidance of excessive increases in real wages and periodic bouts of deflation and thus to the achievement of growth targets scheduled in the national economic plans. Indeed, a bold attempt to achieve *concertation* among the major economic interest groups was made under the sponsorship of the Planning *Commissariat* in 1963–1964, but it failed. In 1969–1970, following the wage explosion of 1968 and the ensuing deflation and devaluation, the Pompidou government introduced a series of innovations—including profit-sharing and two-year contracts providing for grievance adjudication and linking pay to productivity—which are designed to modify labor-market institutions and possibly make them more amenable to restrained wage behavior.

WEST GERMANY

West Germany, like Italy and France, has been popularly regarded as a country relatively immune from inflationary pressures generated autonomously by collective-bargaining institutions. Moreover, it has been subjected to some apparently inflationary and highly visible market influences. Yet unlike Italy, where there have been no really systematic attempts to develop an incomes policy, and unlike France, where similar attempts have been made but have been concentrated on price restraint. West Germany has been trying to develop an incomes policy which would rely solely on wage guidelines. This policy paradox is heightened in part—but in part resolved—by examination of the nature of the movements of wages and prices in the Federal Republic, of the organization of the country's labor and product markets, and of the rather distinctive thrust of the incomes policy itself.

INCREASED LABOR SCARCITY

At the beginning of the sixties the two main sources of labor for the West German expansion during the previous decade were all but eliminated. These were unemployment and refugees from East Germany. According to the OECD, these two sources combined had supplied annually about a quarter million workers, generally highly

PAY AND PRODUCTIVITY CHANGES
IN WEST GERMANY MANUFACTURING, 1952–1965

	1952-1958		1958-1965	
	Per cent rise p. a.	Rank	Per cent rise p. a.	Rank
Hourly rates	5.7	3 (of 11)	7.2	2 (of 12)
Hourly earnings	6.6	4 (of 13)	8.9	2 (of 13)
Output per manhour	4.7	2 (of 12)	5.5	5.5 (of 13)
Unit labor (earnings) cost	1.8	8 (of 12)	3.2	2.5 (of 13)

SOURCE: Economic Commission for Europe, *Incomes in Postwar Europe: A Study of Policies, Growth and Distribution* (Geneva: United Nations, 1967), Chapter 3, Tables 3.1, 3.2, and table on page 4, Chapter 3.

skilled.[1] The disappearance of these reserves did not put an end to the "German miracle" of extraordinary economic growth. Except in the recession of 1966–1967, growth continued throughout the 1960's; indeed, as the table above indicates, the average annual rate of increase in manufacturing productivity was considerably higher (about 17 per cent) between 1958 and 1965 than it had been between 1952 and 1958. However, the increase in the rate of rise in wages (about 35 per cent in the case of hourly earnings) was greater still, with the result that unit labor costs rose much more rapidly in the second period than in the first. West Germany's cost experience was not unique, but it was more pronounced than in most other countries: she ranked eighth out of 12 countries with respect to rise in unit labor costs in the 1950's, and was tied for second place (in a field of 13) in 1958–1965. This rise in the Federal Republic's inflationary standing resulted from a rise in her relative rate of

[1]OECD Economic Surveys, *Germany* (Paris: OECD, January 1963), p. 5.

increase in pay and a fall in her relative rate increase in productivity.

The turnabout in the West German labor market, from a condition of net excess supply to a condition of net excess demand in the 1960's is shown dramatically in the OECD chart below. Not until the recession of 1966–1967 did the number of unemployed exceed the number of unfilled job vacancies in the previous decade. Underlying the accelerated pay increase during this period was an extremely low level of unemployment—below 1 per cent between 1960 and 1967. West Germany's *relatively* large decline in the rate of productivity increase was probably also related to the exhaustion of the old reservoirs, for the increased labor force participation by women and migrant labor from southern Europe could not supply labor whose skill levels were comparable to those possessed by German immigrants and unemployed workers.

Inflation generated out of this changed demand-supply relationship is hardly the type of ailment against which incomes policy has been prescribed as a remedy. Might the emergence of incomes policy in West Germany in the 1960's therefore be provisionally regarded as at least in part a political reflex to the phenomenon of inflation?

DOCILE UNIONS AND TOUGH EMPLOYERS

The political-reflex hypothesis of German incomes policy would not appear to be contradicted by the results of an examination of the working of the country's collective-bargaining system. Bargaining is largely

Number of Registered Unemployed and Jobs Vacant, West Germany

SOURCE: OEEC Statistical Bulletins, General Statistics; OECD, *Main Economic Indicators.*

organized on a regional and industrial basis. Structurally, German trade unionism resembles Swedish unionism in its emphasis on industrial, rather than craft or occupational organization; there are sixteen industrial unions, and these conduct collective bargaining largely at the regional or state level. Unlike the Swedish model, however, the individual industrial unions in Germany are independent of the central federation, the Deutscher Gewerkschaftsbund (DGB), to which they belong; in this respect, the German unions resemble the traditional American pattern of collective bargaining conducted exclusively by or within autonomous national unions. Since the industrial form of organization has generally been regarded as more conducive to efficient utilization of labor in the plant and less resistant to technological displacement than craft unionism, it is doubtful that the relative—but not absolute—slowdown in the rate of increase in German productivity in the sixties can be attributed to German unionism.

On the other hand, the German unions are better organized for collective bargaining within product or labor markets and thus to generate conventional "cost-push" movements than are the French or Italian union movements. The largely blue-collar membership of the sixteen national unions represents about a third of the labor force; another 8 to 10 per cent is accounted for by affiliates of a white-collar federation and by a few independent unions. Moreover, under a 1949 statute a collective-bargaining agreement in a partly covered industry can be legally extended to the entire industry if both parties to the agreement so desire, if the agreement covers at least half the employees in the industry, and if extension is regarded as in the public interest by the Minister of Labor. However, it might be argued that the German system's structural potential for cost-push has not been fully realized. There have certainly been two strongly inhibiting forces at work: the apparent inhibition of the union leadership and membership and the resistance of the employers.

German unionism has had a widespread reputation for docility. According to one interesting theory, this docility reflects a proletarian feeling of inferiority fed by an educational system which has discriminated against working-class children by sending only a minor proportion of the elementary school population through secondary school and university education.[2] But a probably more important reason is a deep-rooted fear of both inflation and unemployment which is found in all sections of the population. The German inflation after World War I and the ensuing period of high unemployment, which preceded the rise of the Nazis, are still vivid memories

[2] Murray Edelman and R. W. Fleming, *The Politics of Wage-Price Decisions: A Four-Country Analysis* (Urbana: University of Illinois Press, 1965), pp. 83–86.

to older, Social Democratic union leaders. Their generation, due to the loss of life in World War II, was disproportionately represented in the top union ranks during the fifties and sixties[3] and some of them feel that the Social Democrats and trade unions had been partly responsible for that early inflation and therefore for the economic and political catastrophes of the next twenty years. Moreover, adult Germans still recall the immediate postwar inflation and the drastic (although highly effective) currency reform of 1948. And the contraction of 1966–1967 revived memories of unemployment among the middle aged and shocked the young, when, after a half-decade of excess demand and tight full employment, employers abandoned their habitual reluctance to lay off domestic employees as well as imported foreign labor. This helps to explain how, in 1967 and 1968, there were concerted attempts to insert provisions into the long-term (four- to five-year) nonwage agreements requiring advance notice of dismissal, educational leaves, and temporary rate maintenance and severance pay as a protection against the inroads of automation.[4] (It may also help to explain why the government called the comprehensive Manpower Development Law of 1967 a "labor law for the age of automation"—and why the law provides subsidies for employers for "short-time compensation" up to full pay for employees affected by temporary shutdowns caused by "structural changes," and the like, why it requires employers to give at least twelve months' advance notice of such technological or structural changes, and why it provides wage subsidies (of up to 60 per cent) for the hiring of older workers.[5])

[3] *Ibid.*, p. 83.

[4] U.S. Bureau of Labor Statistics, *Labor Developments Abroad,* September 1967, p. 15.

[5] *Ibid.*, November 1969, pp. 1–4.

It might be argued that the Germans were essentially following—although also expanding—American collective-bargaining and public policies, which were also undertaken on the premise that automation did and would cause widespread unemployment; however, prevailing levels of unemployment in the United States in the fifties and early sixties were much higher than unemployment levels in West Germany in the sixties.

Partly because of their real fear of unemployment, German unionists have tended to be leery of inflationary wage increases. Not unlike the Italians in this respect, German workers and their leaders are aware that wage increases might well be followed and neutralized by price increases and that the latter might well be followed by deflation and unemployment. Edelman and Fleming reported the results of a 1963 poll in Baden-Württemberg in which 79 per cent of the workers believed that any wage increase would be completely offset by price inflation.[6] In a more recent poll a high proportion of workers claimed that they would be willing to settle for no wage increase at all if prices could hold stable. Such samplings of opinion about the world in general need not be taken too seriously (especially when they imply acceptance of stability in real wages). The point is that the collective economic behavior of the German unionists seems to have been inhibited by such grass-roots subscription to a cost-push theory of inflation and by apprehension over the outcome.

Reinforcing the alleged inhibiting factors of social diffidence and fear of inflation and unemployment might have been a sense of satisfaction with the rate of personal economic progress. Thus average remuneration per capita in manufacturing rose by 134 per cent between

[6] Edelman and Fleming, *op. cit.*, p. 119.

1953 and 1964, a considerably higher rate of increase than occurred in Belgium, Italy, Norway, and the United Kingdom. The average wage earner got his share of the German miracle; he never had it so good—and what is more important—he had probably never expected to have it so good. An OEEC group of experts had drawn (possibly overdrawn) this inference: "Clearly the incentive and ability of organized labour to push up the rate of wage advance to the point where it endangers price stability is likely to be less when the permissible rate of wage increase is 5 per cent than when it is 3 per cent."[7]

But West German employers have also played a role in restraining union behavior. They are generally regarded as better organized and as having been in a consistently stronger bargaining position than the unions. Although bargaining is conducted autonomously on an industry-wide or regional level, the central employers' association (the BDA) has a special strike fund out of which member firms might be compensated for fixed expenses and salaries of white-collar workers. This is of special advantage to smaller member firms, but even more important to them is the practice of holding wages at levels which small-scale firms can afford to pay. The larger and the more efficient firms also benefit from this system, for it has in practice left most of them with considerable discretionary control over local pay supplements and thus over plant wage structures. Sometimes such wage drift items are subject to informal bargaining between management and the works council, although the latter are not supposed to negotiate over pay unless specifically authorized to do so under the terms of national contracts. The plant works councils, which are not union organs, have been no match for management in such negotiations.

[7] W. Fellner, *et al., The Problem of Rising Prices* (Paris: The Organization for European Economic Co-operation, 1961), p. 355.

Although unions are involved in some plant bargaining, they (like unions elsewhere in Europe) have for the most part been trying in vain to extend their influence down to the shop floor and thus control pay structure. They want to incorporate the nonnegotiated premiums, bonuses, and so on, into the legally enforceable formal wage structure, to make the latter more uniform by industrywide job classification (as in the steel industry in the United States), and also to decentralize bargaining down to the plant level.[8] Their failure to make much progress along these lines suggests that wage drift in West Germany does not reflect significant cost-push.

This hypothesis is supported by two aspects of the behavior of wage drift: First, evidence of a systematic negative relationship between wage drift and the percentage change in wage rates[9] suggests that the former is largely employer determined. Second, German employers have taken advantage of the scope for reduction in drift which is provided (a) by the restriction of protected legal status to negotiated rates, and (b) by a weakening in demand. Thus in the recession of 1966–1967 wage drift was negative; pay above the union scale was actually cut.[10]

WAGE DETERMINATION AND PRICE-SETTING BEHAVIOR

The nature of union-management relationships as well as changes in sources of labor supply suggest that move-

[8] Economic Commission for Europe, *Incomes in Post-War Europe: A Study of Policies, Growth and Distribution* (Geneva: United Nations, 1967), Chapter 4, pp. 26–27; and H. Markmann, "Incomes Policy in Germany," *British Journal of Industrial Relations*, November 1965, p. 333.

[9] Fellner, *op. cit.*, p. 356 (equation 6).

[10] U.S. Bureau of Labor Statistics, *Labor Developments Abroad*, May 1968, p. 10.

ments in money wages in the Federal Republic should reflect the dominant influence of conditions of labor demand relative to supply. The usual statistical proxy for those conditions is the rate of unemployment, but a German study, using annual data for the period 1949 to 1966 found no significant correlation between wage changes and the unemployment rate.[11] On the other hand, a more detailed Canadian study of quarterly data for the period 1954–I to 1965–II indicated that unemployment is an important determinant of wage change. It also found that wages have been particularly sensitive to unemployment rates only below 3 per cent and speculated that wage insensitivity at higher rates reflected extensive and variable employment of foreign labor.[12] As a result, swings in the demand for labor are not reflected sensitively in changes in the unemployment rate.

The statistical significance of the price-change variable in the equation and the economic significance of the relationships involving a time trend and dummy variables are also open to question. A "causal" relationship running from price changes to wage changes is frequently—

[11] W. G. Hoffman, "Die 'Phillips-Kurve' in Deutschland," *Kyklos*, No. 2, 1969.

[12] R. G. Bodkin, E. P. Bond, G. L. Reuber, and T. R. Robinson, *Price Stability and High Employment: The Options for Canadian Economic Policy* (Ottawa: The Economic Council of Canada, 1966), pp. 250–253. The estimating equation in this study is:

$$\dot{W}_t = 7.99 + \underset{(2.65)}{2.17\, U_t^{-1}} + \underset{(1.91)}{1.23\, \dot{P}_t} - \underset{(2.10)}{0.32\, \dot{W}_{t-4}}$$

$$- \underset{(2.64)}{27.87\, \frac{1}{t}} - \underset{(2.51)}{0.08\, \text{DUM}\cdot t} \qquad R^2 = .49$$

in which U^{-1} is the reciprocal of the unemployment rate, $\dot{P}$ is the rate of change of consumer prices, $\frac{1}{t}$ is the reciprocal of the time trend, DUM·t is a variable taking the value zero through 1961 and increasing linearly thereafter, and the t statistics are in parenthesis.

although it should not necessarily be—interpreted as reflecting the cost-push influence of unions attempting to compensate for or anticipate changes in the cost of living. The OEEC study referred to earlier concluded that, during the 1950's, "the influence of previous increases in the cost of living seems to have been rather modest," but the econometric analysis of the longer period obtains a high, if not unquestionably reliable, estimate of the coefficient of the price-change variable.

Two other findings of this analysis might also be interpreted as possible evidence of the existence of cost-push forces in even the West German system of wage determination. The significance of the trend variable suggests here (as in France) that the wage adjustment relationship was displaced upward over the decade beginning in the mid-fifties, although at a declining rate. The second finding is the significance of the DUM•t variable in the equation quoted above. This study used dummy-time as well as standard dummy variables to test for the effectiveness of incomes policy beginning in 1962 in the United States, Britain, France, and Sweden, as well as in West Germany. But West Germany did not originate an incomes policy at the time—although it was moving in that direction, following a spectacularly unsuccessful effort in 1960. Thus the statistical significance of the German dummy variable suggested to the authors that unspecified phenomena other than incomes policy might have been responsible for the significance of the variables in France, Britain, and the United States—countries which did inaugurate or change such policies at the time.[13] On the other hand, might the significance of the German dummy variable, taken together with the

[13] Bodkin, pp. 250–251.

significant price-change and trend variables, suggest that the German unions could after all exert an appreciable push against apparently strong employer resistance but at the same time allow their political opponents in office to strike a responsive chord when they warned of the dangers of inflation and unemployment?

One might sketch a model consistent with these hypotheses. It would be a model of bilateral monopoly, with strong elements of discretionary pricing in the product as well as the labor markets. Some German economists regard the pricing policies of large-scale industry in their country as predominantly cost-determined; this is in part a heritage of the system of price control practiced under the Nazi regime, when the government was the major purchaser of their output. Thus it is believed that when even firms in the export sector have found their costs lagging behind the costs of their foreign competitors, they responded mainly by expanding output rather than by raising prices. It also helps to explain why, even under industrywide bargaining, German employers have apparently offered more determined resistance to wage claims than, say, the British for whom industrywide bargaining seems to have lessened the will to resist. It is also incompatible with the type of wage determination envisaged under the Aukrust model, discussed in connection with the smaller and more "open" Scandinavian economies, according to which wage increases are granted with relative ease in the export sectors and are then forced up elsewhere.

Instead, German price behavior suggests a model of "transient monopoly power," set forth by Phelps and Winter, in which the firm hesitates to raise its price in full response to an increase in demand, out of fear of becoming less competitive.[14] And the wage behavior of German employers calls to mind Duesenberry's short-run monopsonist, reluctant to raise wages in the face of increasing demand and a supply of labor so inelastic that the cost of attracting extra labor—including raising the pay of the existing work force—would be much greater than the wage rate required for that purpose.[15]

The price-behavior model is not inconsistent with West Germany's low rate of price increase—both with respect to exports and domestic expenditure—between the early fifties and the early sixties (1953–1964), relative to price increases in other European countries.[16] But the model of wage behavior does not square so easily with the fact that, as the table "Pay and Productivity Changes" suggests, the rise in unit labor costs in West Germany was not much below the average in Europe during the fifties, despite the second highest rate of increase in productivity and despite relatively heavy unemployment and heavy in-migration of high-quality, German-speaking laborers. (The latter two conditions per se made for a highly elastic, rather than inelastic, supply of labor.) Nor do relatively low rates of price increase and relatively high rates of increase in unit cost—a combination which, according to the United Nations report, "argues a marked fall in profit margins"—suggest either exceptional union weakness or exceptional union inhibition. The latter point, however, can be accommodated in a model in which unions are driven to push up costs by a prior rise

[14] See E. S. Phelps, "The New Microeconomics of Inflation and Employment Theory," *American Economic Review,* May 1969, pp. 155–157.

[15] J. S. Duesenberry, *Business Cycles and Economic Growth* (New York: McGraw-Hill, 1958), p. 304.

[16] Economic Commission for Europe, *op. cit.,* Chapter 2, tables on pp. 3–6.

in the cost of living. But a rise in the cost of living sufficient to overcome union apprehensions must be introduced as at least in part a *deus ex machina,* assuming the noninflationary proclivities of German businessmen. In fact, Germans frequently referred to their inflation as "imported" and associated with a persistent tendency toward surplus in the balance of payments (which of course is not a phenomenon wholly independent of German pricing behavior). And so we have a degree of "spontaneous" wage inflation induced by a demand-generated price inflation. Then, once demand conditions permit, domestic enterprises respond to the rise in labor costs as an appropriate signal for raising prices.

To be qualified as a cost-push supplement to the strong demand influences which have played on the West German economy, this sketch would require much more careful analytic exploration and also much more hard confirmatory evidence than is now available. We have thought it useful, however, to refer to these rather unorthodox influences, not in order to explain away ambiguous signals emanating from econometric analysis, but because the German approach to incomes policy seems more understandable in the light of such influences. They help to explain, for example, why economists as well as central bankers and politicians should have prescribed incomes policy for an economy subject to such strong demand pulls and governed by an ethos of laissez-faire in the postwar period. They also help to explain why incomes policy should not have emphasized price restraint in Germany as it has in France, where there is also a high degree of oligopoly and administered pricing but where the oligopolists have failed to achieve a reputation for outstanding self-restraint.

Finally, they make more understandable some interesting peculiarities of the incomes policy which has emerged in the Federal Republic.

GERMAN INCOMES POLICY: INCENTIVES TO RESTRAINT

The first attempt at wage restraint occurred in January 1960 when, at the request of Chancellor Adenauer, Bundesbank President Blessing issued a memorandum calling for a general wage guidepost of 4 per cent in 1961. The Blessing memorandum was cautiously supported by the employers' federation which took pains to state that additional compensation for cost-of-living increases (which Blessing did not mention) would be inflationary and that unions could not be compensated for any past lag of negotiated rates behind the growth of over-all productivity.[17] The unions initially responded that any guideline should include price control and permit labor to increase its share of national income.

The 4 per cent guidepost was based on the increase in productivity forecast for 1961. In fact, the 1961 productivity increase turned out to be 6.4 per cent, and Blessing was severely criticized by economists as well as unions for his conservative underprediction of productivity growth and also for ignoring the cost of living in his calculation of the "room" for pay increases. In any event, earnings (including wage drift) rose by 9 per cent in 1961 and the experience with "underpredicted" productivity growth soured the unions on the reliability of government-formulated guidelines.

Partly as a result of this experience, a bill to establish

[17] OECD Economic Surveys, *Germany,* January 1963, p. 20.

a Council of Economic Experts, to be independent of the government, was introduced in the summer of 1962. In August 1963 the bill was finally approved, providing for a seven man council of academicians who are authorized to analyze existing policy, and present alternatives for future policy, but who are not supposed to make recommendations. However, in the course of presenting alternatives in its annual reports, the council has implicitly made recommendations; and for incomes policy there have been a series of explicit proposals.[18]

In its first report, at the beginning of 1965, the council called for wage and price restraint, but it disavowed the rigorous linkage with productivity which the Blessing memorandum had called for. (In this connection it advocated the adoption of fiscal measures which would create incentives for a higher rate of employee savings.) However, the council has always been expansionist in outlook, and it regarded the costs of a restrictionist monetary policy as unacceptable because it induced both deflation and a self-defeating inflow of foreign funds. As the 1964–1965 boom peaked, the council anticipated a characteristic wage push in response to the "imported" price inflation. Whereupon the council actively encouraged "concerted action." It met with union and management leaders; and the unions agreed to accept a productivity guideline for wages, provided that the government take effective steps to restrain demand by appropriate fiscal policy and also to counter inflationary forces of external origin. The council had always strongly favored a more active contracyclical role for fiscal policy,

[18] For an interesting comparison of the German Council of Economic Experts with the U.S. Council of Economic Advisers, see Henry Wallich, "The American Council of Economic Advisers and the German Sachverstaendigenrat: A Study in the Economics of Advice," *Quarterly Journal of Economics*, August 1968.

but the Erhard government, in an election year, chose to cut income taxes and then to allow expenditures to rise beyond budgeted limits. This increased the burden on monetary policy, and there ensued a contraction, complete with profit squeeze and a 4 per cent rise in consumer prices. According to some versions, the bank tackled its task with undue alacrity, and the monetary stringency which it imposed reflected a punitive intent to chastise both the government (for fiscal irresponsibility) and the unions (for irresponsible wage policies).

With a new coalition in office, including a Social Democratic economist (Dr. Schiller) as Minister of Economic Affairs, the council pushed ahead with incomes policy proposals. It published a wage norm for 1966, calling for maximum increases of 5.9 per cent, except in sectors experiencing "an above-average shortage of labor." This norm was calculated after an estimated increase in earnings resulting from movements in employment out of low-paid sectors and into high-paid sectors had been charged against the "room" for pay increases provided not only by an estimated rise in output per man-hour, of 4 per cent, but also in consumer prices, of 2 per cent. According to the United Nations report cited above, "This formulation, which provides for the lagged effect of price pressures already in the system, represents a certain advance toward realism in relation to 'norms' laid down in some other countries."[19] The council did not accord allowance for expected increases in living costs parity in principle with productivity growth; this was in apparent deference to governmental opposition.

[19] Economic Commission for Europe, *op. cit.*, Chapter 4, p. 27. The council also allowed for an expected improvement in the terms of trade.

But the government, under the leadership of its Minister for Economic Affairs, was willing to encourage the council in its efforts to obtain concerted action. In announcing its intention to plan for growth and price stability, the government endorsed a statement by the council that "a policy of controlled expansion combining growth with stabilization is practicable only in connection with a suitable wage policy." And this objective, it added, could be obtained only through agreement between the authorities responsible for economic policy and the parties to collective bargaining, not only on wages but also on such matters as investment and price policies, balance of trade, and the distribution of income and wealth. Accordingly, in June 1966 the council asked the parties to specify the conditions under which they would support the government's stabilization policy for 1967.

The results naturally fell short of concerted perfection, but the German effort was a considerable improvement over the French "dialogue of mutes" in 1963–1964. The BDA, representing the employers, remained opposed to the cost-of-living supplement, and later took the position that any guidelines should recognize that the existence of wage drift implied that the noninflationary standard for the rate of negotiated wage increases should be *less* than the rate of growth of productivity.[20] (The BDA did not repeat this argument the following year when, given the existence of *negative* drift, the logical consequence of their position was that negotiated rates should increase *more* rapidly than productivity.)

The union side was more receptive to the positions taken by Schiller and the council, although it insisted on the maintenance of free collective bargaining. Their

[20] U.S. Bureau of Labor Statistics, *Labor Developments Abroad,* May 1967, pp. 1–2.

response reflected not only bargaining weakness aggravated by the current recession (1966–1967) but also their ingrained economic caution and political loyalty to the Social Democratic side in the coalition government. In 1967, the number of unemployed exceeded the number of unfilled job vacancies for the first time since 1959, but even before this occurrence the council noted a considerable slowdown in the rate of wage increase. It also noted that the unions made no serious attempts to enforce their wage demands by striking and that they accepted postponement of previously negotiated reductions in hours of work. In the first nine months of 1966, collectively bargained rates were only 6 per cent above those prevailing in the first nine months of 1965; and in the comparable period in 1967, the rate of increase had dropped to 3.6 per cent—the lowest in ten years.

The council's target rate of increase in wages and supplementary benefits combined was 8.5 per cent over the two-year period 1968–1969. This was based on an estimated rise in productivity of 6 per cent in 1968 and 4.4 per cent in 1969; it also allowed for scheduled increases in employer contributions to social insurance, increasing unit capital costs, anticipated drift, and tax change. This guideline was justified not only as noninflationary but also as necessary to secure targeted increases in consumption, capacity utilization, and, consequently, investment. A sound wage policy, according to the council's 1967 report, should reconcile management's concern over wages as costs with the union view of wages as purchasing power. Consistent with these principles, the council suggested further that, in addition to the 8.5 per cent guide for wage development, collective agreements should provide for wage adjustments or contract terminations if the productivity and price assumptions underlying the guide do not obtain. Specifically, it was suggested that if productivity growth is slower than anticipated, employers should be able to postpone some contract provisions, whereas if productivity growth is unusually rapid, unions should be able to obtain larger increases. The report also suggests that escalation clauses should guarantee compensation if price trends are greater than anticipated.[21]

When Dr. Schiller shaved down the wage guidepost on the basis of an estimated increase in productivity of only 4 per cent in 1968, the council objected on the grounds that it would unduly lengthen the lag of wages behind prices and thus invite a bout of cost-push inflation after capacity had become fully utilized. The council itself thus appeared to take the purchasing power seriously, at least in part: without a sufficiently large rise in wages, consumption would lag, too many resources would be diverted to exports, and price inflation would thereby be "imported." The idea is to time money-wage increases correctly.

But if this formulation of wage policy was intended to be a sop to the unions as well as a prescription for non-inflationary expansion, it proved to be an embarrassingly generous gesture. For the unions did not particularly side with the council against Schiller; if anything, the unions were not prepared to set their sights as high as the government would have approved. They argued against big wage increases on two grounds. First, prices had been stable, so real wage rates were not being eroded. Second, their members were being laid off for the first time in almost a decade; and if the union leaders negotiated big increases under such conditions, they might well be denounced for endangering jobs. Not that the unionists were prepared to abandon the purchasing power theory;

[21] *Ibid.*, May 1968, pp. 9–11.

they were opposed to the pay cuts which showed up as negative drift in 1967, and they supported concerted action and the council with the slogan "No negative wage policy!"

AN INCOMES POLICY FOR A NEW GENERATION?

The form of wages policy developed by the West Germany's Council of Economic Experts was tied in more explicitly to stabilization and growth policies than the policies in any other countries dealt with in this study, with the possible exception of the Netherlands. As a result it could offer a more powerful positive incentive to compliance, in the form of a specified rise in real wage incomes corresponding to the permissible rise in money wages. Where incomes policy was propounded elsewhere as a necessary condition for achieving a faster growth in real wages, in Germany it was set forth as a sufficient condition as well. There it appeared that this guarantee could be underwritten by three conditions. The first was the persistence of an underlying tendency toward surplus on international account. In Germany, at least until the revaluation of October 1969 (and possibly thereafter as well), this surplus was associated with an undervalued currency; and, to some extent, the council's incomes policy—with a wage norm that served as a minimum as well as a maximum—served as an imperfect substitute for the revaluation which the council pressed (and persuaded) both the Social Democrats and the unions to espouse as essential to price stability. The export surplus emerged strongly in the recovery in the second half of 1967 and remained substantial after the 1969 revaluation.

Less well fulfilled were the other two conditions

underlying the potential effectiveness of incomes policy in West Germany. One of these is price stability and the other is the stability of the trade-union movement. Without price stability, one can insert cost-of-living adjustments into wage guidelines only by running the risk of sanctioning destabilizing wage increases. This is a risk which the government was reluctant to incur even when prices were quite stable. However, following relative stability in 1967 and 1968, the cost of living began to rise quite rapidly (by German standards) in the second quarter of 1969, reaching an annual rate of 3.5 per cent early in the first quarter of 1970. The council forecast a price rise of at least 3 per cent and possibly 4 or 5 per cent, in 1970; and they warned that such increases—resulting from insufficient revaluation—might trigger "dangerously exorbitant wage demands." (Larger wage increases might also have been predicted on the basis of an increase in the excess of vacancies over unemployment since the second quarter of 1968 as well as the decline in unemployment to around 1 per cent, but this is the type of relationship which incomes policy is supposed to loosen.)

More ominous than price behavior for the future of incomes policy have been recent manifestations of a change in the economic mentality of the West German worker. Such an eventuality had been regarded as remote, as one might well imagine, notwithstanding the emergence of two possible symptoms of destabilization in German industrial relations.

The first of these concerns "codetermination," an early German innovation in worker "participation" in the management of industry. In Germany's stratified society, the issue of codetermination is an important issue of employee status, and provision for participation in the upper echelons of management and works councils at the plant level were set up in a series of laws in the early fifties. The strongest participation arrangements exist in the coal and steel industries operating under the Codetermination Law of 1951, which provides for equal labor and management representation on supervisory boards of companies and for the appointment of the personnel director (one of three managing directors of the firm) by the unions. Most other industries are covered by a 1952 law which provides for representation on the supervisory board but not on the board of management. Moreover, unions have not been able to incorporate most of the local works councils into their machinery, as we have noted above.

Following complaints from some of the national unions, the DGB is now seeking legislation that would extend the codetermination procedures which now cover the coal and steel industries to four hundred major firms in other industries.[22] The unions face determined employer opposition (on the grounds that the proposed change would eliminate the "balance" in German industrial relations) so that the outcome is in doubt. However, based on the record, an extension of codetermination might not have been regarded as an economically destabilizing development; for, even in coal and steel, which the DGB regard as their model for emulation, the labor directors are paid by management, are pledged to secrecy regarding high-level managerial decisions, and have tended "to grow away from the group that put them in office and instead to identify with their new colleagues."[23] For example, the economists on the council encountered difficulty in selling the union leadership on

[22] *Ibid.*, November 1968, p. 9.
[23] Edelman and Fleming, *op. cit.*, p. 122.

the merits of revaluation because labor directors in the large export firms had been convinced by their managerial colleagues that revaluation would cause serious unemployment in their industries.

The other possible danger signal has been a tendency for union membership, relative to the work force, to stagnate. While total employment increased by 42.2 per cent between 1951 and 1966, membership in the DGB rose only 10.6 per cent. The DGB's share of the wage and salary work force declined from 38 per cent to 30 per cent.[24] This too, however, was not regarded as an economic danger signal. On the contrary, it could be viewed as a development consistent with the deeply ingrained caution of the German workers. As Edelman and Fleming put it:

> The German unions have had to cope in the postwar years with a membership that has often had reason to doubt that its good fortune could be attributed to unions. Worse, the members have been afraid that militant union action would do them more harm than good.[25]

However, in September of 1969, more than a million West German workers startled the world, their compatriots, and possibly themselves as they launched a series of wildcat strikes for higher pay. They might have caught the fever from the French and Italian strikes of 1968 and 1969, or they might have contracted "British disease" of much earlier origin. A younger generation was heavily represented in their ranks, with no discernible sense of inferiority and inhibition based upon a discriminatory educational or social system and with much shorter memories of inflation and unemployment.

[24] U.S. Bureau of Labor Statistics, *Labor Developments Abroad,* August 1968, pp. 4–5.

[25] *Op. cit.*, p. 119.

And if, as suggested above, German workers had been restrained in their collective behavior by satisfaction with their economic progress as individuals, they might well have learned to take rapid progress for granted, so that the appetites have now grown faster than the eating. (According to one economic theory of inflation, workers are supposed to respond initially to unanticipated wage increases by increasing their willingness to take and stay on jobs, but then, as they come to expect a going rate of wage increase, they become more choosy and, by reducing their collective supply of labor, tend to drive wages up more rapidly.) Indeed the deflationary shock of 1967–1968, by depressing the rate of economic progress below the rate which they had come to expect, might have produced a worker reaction exactly opposite to what the monetary authorities at the Bundesbank had intended and anticipated. In a similar vein, the Economist Intelligence Unit reported, a tight labor market, "coupled with the changing mentality of the workers, who no longer worry too much over price increases as long as their standard of living keeps rising."[26]

The wildcat movement took the union leaders by surprise. Indeed, the strikes were directed against the unions as much as the employers, as had been the case in France and Italy and as was later true in Sweden. At least in this later period apathy toward unionism did not necessarily imply worker docility after all, but rather worker impatience with union docility. Otto Brenner, the head of the giant metal workers' union and for years an exponent of Socialist opposition as opposed to American-style "business unionism," was caught off guard when the steel workers demanded nullification of

[26] Economist Intelligence Unit, *Quarterly Economic Review, Germany, No. 1, 1970* (March 1970), Summary page.

their contract. Brenner had been trying to cooperate with Dr. Schiller's price stabilization policy, now that the Social Democrats were in office. And so, prodded from below, the unions hastily raised their bargaining sights. Before September, negotiated increases in wage rates had been averaging 5 to 7 per cent; the wildcats triggered off settlements of 10 per cent and more, many of them before the termination of the contract period. Actual earnings per employee, including wage drift and other payments, rose at an annual rate of 14 to 15 per cent on a January 1960 to January 1970 basis. This compared with the generous estimate of 9½ to 10½ per cent in the annual economic report of 1970.[27]

Thus the climate of incomes policy in the Federal Republic apparently suffered an abrupt deterioration. What had seemed to be a uniquely favorable institutional environment was transformed into a situation which, neither favorable nor unique, was characterized by a trade-union movement whose central officers were disposed to cooperation but many of whose rank and file—or potential rank and file—had loudly repudiated their moderate (and older) leaders. In many cases, employers looked to the works councils, rather than the unions, to end wildcats and, in their anxiety to settle, did not even dock the strikers' pay. The response of the Social Democratic government was more predictable: it proposed profit-sharing and more employee participation in management. The response of the bank was familiar to the Germans themselves: it pushed up interest rates.

The response of the "wise men" on the council, however, was consistent in terms of their own policy but novel in the annals of incomes policy. Their policy had

[27] *Ibid.*, p. 10; also *Quarterly Economic Review, No. 4, 1969*, p. 10.

always aimed at translating money wage increases into real wage increases; so long as these increases remained on target, they would be consistent with the achievement or maintenance of full employment and price stability. If, however, money wage increases turn out to exceed the norm and if the authorities nevertheless determine to underwrite the employment goal, then prices must be inflated more rapidly than money wages. The fall in real wage rates is an impetus to further inflation and frustration of incomes policy. Their conclusion is that, if the unions wish to exercise control over the money-wage level to redistribute income in favor of wages, they should be allowed to do so—and to pay the price in terms of employment. If public authority has no effective instrument for controlling the rate of increase in money wages, it ought not to make full use of employment-determining instruments which it does have at hand. It must retreat from the goal of full employment, or at least make explicit that, since the private parties retain some discretionary control over the movement of money wages, they must accept responsibility for the level of unemployment. This is not unlike the nonpolicy adumbrated by former Secretary of Labor George Shultz in the Nixon administration, when he told union and management groups that if they negotiated excessively high settlements they would suffer the consequences in terms of sales and jobs later on. The administration would not bail them out by shifting demand curves outward as soon as the private groups began to climb up them. The essential difference from this approach is that, in the West German case, the authorities are prepared to shine a "guiding light," illuminating the wage route—in both money and real terms—leading to both destinations: price stability and full employment. But both approaches are based on a central assumption, and one that is far from firm: that the citizenry will allow the government to engage in this washing of hands.

CONCLUSION

Studies of the behavior of the West German economy and labor market institutions during the postwar period invariably conclude that labor-market and product-market inflation has been of a classic excess-demand variety and that the German labor movement has never been sufficiently aggressive to counter the aims of the well-organized German employers who appear to have discretionary pricing power in many sectors. Recent statistical evidence is not uniformly consistent with this scenario. During the sixties wages appear to have increased more rapidly than one would have predicted on the basis of past relations between wage inflation, price inflation, and the unemployment rate; and the combination of a relatively high rate of increase in unit labor costs, with a relatively low rate of price increase implied that the profit margins of German employers narrowed relative to margins in neighboring countries.

With the scope of potential effectiveness of incomes policy somewhat uncertain, the German government has generally been reluctant to take the lead in formulating a policy. The one exception to this statement occurred in the early sixties and was based on an underestimate of predicted productivity growth and rendered ineffective by actual experience. Instead, a body of independent academic economists, the Council of Economic Experts, have since 1965 evolved an approach to incomes policy in successive annual reports on economic conditions. The essence of the council's idea is to determine a rate of increase of real wages which is consistent with short-run stability and long-run growth objectives and to specify a formula which will generate that real wage increase, whatever the behavior of other influential variables. Only a money-wage guideline is specified, but the magnitude of the guideline depends on the rate of price increase as well as the rate of growth of labor productivity and other developments affecting employers' costs or workers' disposable income. A recent version suggested that the government should not use monetary and fiscal tools to maintain its employment objectives if actual money-wage increases are inconsistent with the real-wage guideline. The government would thus presumably pursue the aggregative policies necessary to guarantee the equilibrium rate of employment consistent with the guide but let the parties bear the employment and output consequences of violating the guide. As yet no (sectoral) exceptions have been specified, perhaps because the council's approach to guidelines has not yet been adopted by the government.

If West German government officials have not been completely persuaded by the proposed guidelines they have willingly adopted "concerted action," the main administrative arrangement introduced by the council. Informal meetings between officials of the government, employer associations, and union federations have on occasion resulted in modifications in labor contracts, if not government stabilization policies. However, even this arrangement may be a casualty of the new militancy among German rank and file which surfaced in late 1969. What lasting effects this phenomenon will have on the relation between union leadership, rank and file, employers, and the government is difficult to predict at present, although the potential for administering an incomes policy through the bargaining institutions clearly seems reduced.

ITALY

With the exception of an emergency freeze on wages and prices in 1946–1947, serious interest in incomes policy did not develop in Italy until 1963. There are two major reasons why the issue did not arise during the previous decade. First, the existence of a "dual economy" enabled the rapidly industrializing North (as well as other European countries) to draw on large reserves of labor in the rural and underdeveloped South. The combination of an elastic labor supply and extensive foreign aid made it possible for Italy to combine a rapid rate of economic growth with relatively moderate price increases and a generally satisfactory balance-of-payments position during the 1950's.[1] Negotiated wage increases always exceeded 5 per cent a year, and locally determined wage drift made for still larger increases in earnings. Nevertheless, rates of increase in earnings were always less than increases in productivity, until late 1961.

The second reason was the economic weakness of Italian unionism throughout the fifties. The three major Italian labor federations, CGIL, CISL, and UIL have

[1] The per cent increase in the CPI for 1953–1960, 16 per cent, was exceeded by all other countries in this survey except Germany, which experienced a 13 per cent increase. The 1953–1959 per cent change in the implicit price index for total final output in the national accounts statistics was lowest for Italy (7.9 per cent) among the countries surveyed. See William Fellner *et al., The Problem of Rising Prices* (Paris: Organization for European Economic Cooperation, 1961), pp. 89, 113–115.

been strongly tied to the Communist, Christian Democratic, and Social Democratic parties, respectively;[2] and during much of this period preoccupation with political ideological differences minimized their interest and effectiveness in collective bargaining. Collective bargaining consisted largely of the negotiation of national agreements between the central labor federations and a large central employers' federation, Confindustria, which has been interested in the survival of the small-scale and often inefficient firms comprising the bulk of its membership. As a result, the central negotiations established low minimum-wage rates,[3] which were initially differentiated on regional lines. Another distinctive feature of the system has been the importance of automatic escalation. In a feature that is elsewhere approximated only in Denmark (among the countries included in this survey), virtually all Italian contracts have provided for a wage increase of 0.6 per cent for every 1 per cent increase in the cost-of-living index.

This system left the wage level and the wage structures highly responsive to changes in demand and supply. The centrally negotiated minimum rates have always been exceeded by the larger, more efficient, more rapidly growing firms; and to the extent that their wage premiums have been required to attract workers, movements in

[2] The three federations are the Confederazione Generale Italiana del Lavoro, the Confederazione Italiana dei Sindacati Lavoratori, and the Unione Italiana del Lavoro.

[3] Some observers suggest that Italian unions were so weak or disinterested in industrial responsibilities during the first half of the postwar period, that the minimum negotiated wage was what employers thought was just necessary to prevent general social unrest. Moreover, the use of inflated cost figures during negotiations enabled some members of Confindustria to achieve (illegal) negative drift—this, also despite the presence of unions! On these points see Murray Edelman and R. W. Fleming, *The Politics of Wage-Price Decisions* (Urbana: University of Illinois Press, 1965), pp. 32–38.

wage drift were demand-determined. Likewise, as geographic disparities in industrial development narrowed, pressures to reduce the geographic inequalities in minimum rates resulted in a reduction in the number of wage zones from 95 to 13 with a maximum interzone spread of 30 per cent in 1954, and again to 6 with a maximum gap of 20 per cent in 1961.[4]

At the same time, wage movements might have reflected some elements of "push," even in Italy's miraculous fifties. Thus wage drift paid by some large firms reflected a conscious effort to keep unionism in their plants weak and divided. Moreover, part of the drift has been regarded as a form of strike insurance, since, in large-scale, capital-intensive industry, the cost of down time can be extremely high. Finally, automatic escalation can result in wage increases (in response to prior price increases) which would not be generated by current conditions of demand and supply in the labor market.

Nevertheless, the relatively moderate price increases which Italy experienced in the fifties were generally considered to be associated with temporary structural tensions in economic development and predominantly demand-determined. As a result, in Italy (as in Germany), the dominant anti-inflationary instrument has been monetary policy, which was quite successful in coping with transient balance-of-payment difficulties.

THE BASES FOR INCOMES POLICY

This economically happy state of affairs, however, barely survived the fifties. Beginning in the third quarter of 1961, Italy experienced a wage explosion: in the next two years average hourly earnings in manufacturing rose

[4] *Ibid.*, p. 35.

by over one-third, the somewhat slower increase in prices resulted in a profits squeeze, the share of labor in the distribution of national income rose markedly as did consumption spending, and the country experienced a large deficit on current account combined with an outflow of capital.[5] The Bank of Italy restricted credit; this and other deflationary measures led to a recession and a rise in unemployment in 1963–1964. These measures effectively restrained the inflation and exports rose sharply, leading an expansion which began in 1965. However, monetary policy now came to be regarded as a more painful and less efficient instrument than heretofore; and interest in incomes policy became active in various quarters, including notably the Bank of Italy. There were several reasons for this. Some were rooted in controversy over the nature of the wage explosion; others in the response of the economy to the deflationary remedies; and still others in the altered political composition of the government.

The appearance of a cost push mechanism?

There is still some disagreement about the exact causes of the explosion. The official position of the Bank of Italy, which is shared by many Italian economists, is that the explosion resulted from a sudden pushfulness on the part of the unions and that this in turn resulted from new wage agreements as well as the culmination of a number of institutional trends which eroded the customary tranquillity of Italian unions in collective bargaining. By the end of the 1950's, the Italian labor federations began to interest themselves more seriously in the potentialities of collective bargaining as a policy instrument.

[5] See for example, OECD Economic Surveys, *Italy* (Paris: OECD, June 1967), p. 17.

To this end the three major Italian federations began drawing together for policy purposes and (since the mid-sixties) even debated the advisability of merger and of withdrawing union officials from political office. The latter developments are not in themselves relevant to an explanation of the wage developments at the beginning of the decade; but they are manifestations of delayed institutional response to pushfulness which originated earlier and from below.

Another manifestation of grass-roots pushfulness was the movement toward decentralized or "articulated" bargaining. The first departures from completely centralized bargaining occurred in the mid-fifties when the IRI (Instituto per la Ricostruzione Industriale)—one of two large quasi-public holding companies which coordinates a group of large-scale enterprises in which the state has a controlling interest—obtained legislative permission to bargain for companies it controlled. In the 1962 negotiations the unions pushed hard on the issue of plant-level bargaining. IRI, which has steadily been modernizing its industrial-relations practices, settled first, agreeing to a structure which restricted economy-wide (or at least multisector) agreements to broad general issues, provided for the establishment of hours and minimum rates industry by industry, and also for negotiated plant-level agreements covering piece work, productivity bonuses, and related issues. Later, Confindustria agreed to less complete decentralization for its members in the wholly private sector. At the same time, the Christian Democratic unions demanded that plant-level bargaining involve the unions directly, rather than the shop committees which had been dominated by companies in a manner which would be illegal under American labor law. Their demand was not completely granted; but, in any event, this general structural change marked the end of general employer resistance to unionism *per se,* as it did the practical abandonment by the unions of the old ideologically motivated ethic of wage equality.

In support of the hypothesis that the wage explosion of 1961–1963 reflected such institutional and structural changes,[6] various bits of statistical evidence have been cited. Among these are a squeeze on profits which accompanied the wage explosion and the fact that the major component of that upsurge consisted in negotiated increases and raises granted in the public sector under union pressure, while only a minor part reflected the operation of the cost-of-living escalator. In addition, an equation, which is part of an econometric model of the Italian economy and which seeks to account for changes in money wages with reference to the level of unemployment and changes in the cost of living, underpredicted the wage increase in 1962.[7] The fact that this wage increase was greater than could be accounted for on the basis of these generally accepted demand factors alone led the author to speculate that something new had been added to the Italian wage-determining machinery.

Although the profits squeeze is certainly suggestive,

[6] See, for example, Banca D'Italia, *Report for the Year 1961* (abridged version), (Rome, 1962), p. 19, "The rise of the wage level in 1961 was due in part to the renewal of many wage agreements and to the growing practice, for firms to negotiate their own agreements with workers, and in part to the application of new agreements regarding inter-regional wage parity in industry and transport."

Other sources mention without evidence an increased propensity of workers to strike as psychological fears of unemployment were reduced by the growth of the 1950's and reduced employer resistance. See Gino Giugni, "Recent Developments in Collective Bargaining in Italy," *International Labour Review,* April 1965, pp. 280–281.

[7] P. Sylos-Labini, "Prices, Distribution, and Investment in Italy,

this statistical evidence as a whole is hardly conclusive. It is well known that a simple Phillips curve is consistent with virtually any interpretation of inflationary phenomena and that its explanatory variables are imperfect proxies of the forces—of demand, in this case—which they hopefully represent. Thus some Italian economists, while not necessarily interpreting 1961–1963 as a purely demand phenomenon, point out that the accompanying unemployment rate of 3 per cent had been low by earlier Italian postwar standards and could therefore have been counted on to generate an exceptionally high rate of wage inflation. Although large-scale labor reserves, which had previously exerted a dampening effect on wage increases, obviously remained, the large decline in unemployment which occurred in 1961–1963 was associated with shortages in various skilled-labor categories. Such structural shortages could themselves account for exceptionally high wage increases. Finally, it was claimed that the institutional changes discussed above had not yet had time to influence wage developments in 1962–1963.

The verdict of the economic historian is not yet in. But whatever it may be, it is significant for policy (a) that the cost-push view is held by the bank, which holds the levers of monetary policy and is by far the most powerful agent of over-all economic policy in the country; and (b) that even opponents of the cost-push interpretation of the

1951–66," *Quarterly Review, Banco Nazionale del Lavoro,* December 1967. In the model industrial wages are explained by the equation

$$\dot{W} = -0.621 + 18.903\ U^{-1} + 1.198\ \dot{P}$$

in which U is the nonagricultural unemployment rate and $\dot{P}$ is the rate of change of consumer prices. However, these coefficients are estimated by single-equation technique, a serious shortcoming in view of qualitative evidence of particularly strong interdependencies between price and wage changes in the Italian economy.

1961–1963 wage movements share the view that the institutional and structural changes in Italian collective bargaining are of considerable economic significance.

The Diminishing Effectiveness of Monetary Policy in 1963–1965.

The wage explosion of 1961–1963 resulted in a large deficit in the current long-term capital accounts. Deflationary monetary-fiscal policy was effective in restoring the export surplus, but at the cost of higher unemployment. Moreover, the subsequent expansion required the maintenance of relatively low interest levels, which in turn frustrated efforts to restore the importation of foreign capital which had prevailed in the 50's. This has helped to make the Bank of Italy receptive to incomes policy. Its argument runs as follows: The reemergence of an export surplus did not appear to be as effective in stimulating a recovery in domestic production and employment in 1964 as it had been on earlier occasions. This was attributed to wage increases which had the effect of restraining profit margins to the point where domestic investment was made insufficiently profitable. At the same time, the relatively greater rise in Italy's labor costs, coupled with a relatively lower rate of increase in Italian export prices, made foreign investment attractive and thus resulted in deficits in the long-term capital account, which in turn raised interest rates at home. Finally, the high rates of increase in Italian wages in 1961–1963 was attributed to cost-push influences—collective bargaining and automatic wage escalation ("which end by spreading even erratic fluctuations, so that they become irreversible, cumulative").[8] Thus, if incomes policy could restrain the rate of wage rise, it could strengthen the linkage between deflation-induced export surpluses and domestic investment and at the same time help the bank to keep long-term capital at home without resorting to deflationary monetary policy.

The Center-Left Coalition and the Bank.

The existence of the Center-Left coalition government which took office at the beginning of the sixties was originally conducive to the adoption of an incomes policy. Heavy reliance on monetary policy and high interest rates would counter other forces making for a redistribution of income in favor of the wage earners, a development which was favored by the government. The Bank of Italy, under the direction of Dr. Guido Carli, was also sympathetic to the government's aspirations toward growth-cum-redistribution, and it too championed the cause of incomes policy. From the viewpoint of the government, support by the bank in the form of compatible monetary policy would have been essential to the success of any incomes policy. From the viewpoint of the bank, support by a Center-Left government would have been essential. The bank, while by far the strongest center of demand management in the country, has always been remote from the unions and thus would have had little chance of enlisting their cooperation with a policy of wage restraint. It was hoped that the new government, which was closer to the non-Communist unions than its predecessors, might be influential here. And the govern-

[8] See Guido Carli, "Problems of Today," *Review of the Economic Conditions in Italy,* No. 4, 1966, pp. 263–274 (quoted at p. 267); Francesco Masera, "Foreign Trade in the Present Economic Situation of Italy," *Review of the Economic Conditions in Italy,* No. 1, 1966, pp. 22–38; Paoli Baffi, "Les mouvements des salaires et de la balance des paiements dans les récente expérience italienne et internationale," *Moneta e credito,* giugno, 1969, pp. 131–148 (especially, pp. 147–148).

ment, like postwar, growth-oriented left-of-center governments in other lands, tried the approach of encapsulating wage policy in a five-year development plan (1966–1970), which stressed the need to coordinate private wage settlements with public economic policy.[9]

But the unions, newly interested in exploring the potentialities of bargaining, were not too enthusiastic; and so the plan alluded to incomes policy only indirectly, never by name, and gave lip service to the union argument (found in Sweden and the United States as well) that the rate of increase in productivity is a function of the rate of increase in wages, even if the former should limit the latter. In any event, the unions were not overly receptive to the notion of central planning—they were opposed to French-style indicative planning as a capitalist snare and delusion—and hence embedding incomes policy in an over-all plan (as the British and Dutch had done) could not be an effective incentive to acceptance of restraint. As a result, the plan included no guideposts or any provisions for limitation of collective bargaining.

THE EFFECTIVENESS OF INFORMAL ATTEMPTS AT RESTRAINT

Notwithstanding the unions' reluctance to commit themselves to a formal incomes policy, the government was able to induce the unions to postpone the reopening of their contracts in 1965; and the recovery which began that year was marked by relative price stability, a relaxation of the squeeze on profits which had occurred during the wage explosion and subsequent recession, and a good rise in domestic investment.

[9] *Programma economico nazionale per il quinquennio 1966–70.*

The econometric model which underpredicted the wage increase in 1962 overpredicted it in 1965. The latter phenomenon was attributed by Sylos-Labini to "the deliberately moderate policies followed by the Trade Unions [which] were perhaps due to their appreciation, after the 1964 experience, of the negative effects on investment and employment of an excessive increase in wages."[10] But others regarded the smaller wage increases as reflecting not so much the persuasiveness of government as the unionists' recent painful experience of rising unemployment. The Italian unionists seemed to resemble the Germans in that their experience of unemployment in the 1950's heightened their economic sophistication.

Still other economists attributed the restrained wage behavior simply to union-bargaining weakness induced by the 1963–1964 recession, and not to voluntary self-restraint. Thus, the unions sought to postpone renewal of their contracts in 1965; but they did so primarily to wait until a more favorable phase of the cycle would permit them to conclude better three-year contracts. In the end it was the employers who insisted on renewal and held the unions down to a 4 per cent raise. After a year of continuing prosperity, the unions claimed that they had been deceived and proceeded to demand—and obtain—hefty wage increases, and compensated reductions in the work week.

Yet, some maintain that the unions have not yet forgotten the Phillips relationship. In the old days they would

[10] P. Sylos-Labini, *op. cit.*, p. 359. The aggregate model implicit in this statement and the almost exclusive use of monetary policy to stabilize both the domestic and foreign sectors have been criticized by other observers. See Franco Modigliani and Giorgio La Malfa, "Inflation, Balance of Payments Deficit and Their Cure Through Monetary Policy: The Italian Example," *Quarterly Review, Banco Nazionale del Lavoro,* March, 1967.

have defended these claims along purchasing-power lines or simply on the basis of equity. Now they are willing to stipulate that they are not consistent with economic stability in Italy; instead they defend them as revolutionary tactics precisely because they are allegedly inconsistent with the requirements of Italian capitalism! In short, it is claimed in some quarters that the experience of unemployment, reinforced by discussions of incomes policy at the bank and in the government, has been generating in Italy the type of education effect originally claimed on behalf of the *Guideposts* in the United States. But what the Italian experience goes to show is that increased economic sophistication hardly constitutes a sufficient condition for restrained behavior.

OBSTACLES TO THE SUCCESS OF INCOMES POLICY IN ITALY

The public sector.

In various countries—notably in France and Britain—occasional attempts have been made by the government as an employer to enforce incomes policy in the public sector and hope that the example will be followed elsewhere. In Italy where government, operating through the two giant holding companies, IRI and ENI (Ente Nazionale Idrocarburi), has majority holdings in a good deal of heavy industry in the export and growth sectors, there has been some disagreement between the Bank of Italy and the holding companies on the potentiality of this approach. In Italy, according to the bank's argument, the public sectors were actually the worst offenders in the past, for the unions reached agreement first with the the state-controlled companies and then applied this pattern to the private sector. And since IRI and ENI left the employers' confederation, Confindustria, in 1956, they have been under less restraint by the private sector than ever. The influence of the unions on IRI and ENI firms is partly political. But it is also economic: labor-cost ratios tend to be lower in the large government-controlled firms, as a result of which ability to pay is greater while ability to take a shutdown is less.

Some economists in IRI, however, claim that their firms' wages simply reflect firm size and are no higher than those prevailing in large private enterprises like Olivetti and Fiat. Moreover, since the IRI economists take a structural view of inflation in Italy, they argue that their own regional investment policy really constitutes the most appropriate type of incomes policy. (On this issue they are critical of large private firms, such as Fiat, for provoking unrest by concentrating their expansion in the North where worker housing is inadequate and where the working environment is not responsive to the needs of workers fresh off the farms.) Thus, at this writing, there has not yet been an official attempt to administer an incomes policy through the state holding companies.

Price controls.

In view of the extremely high responsiveness of wages to price changes,[11] the absence of any visibly effective price policy would appear to militate against the long-run success of any policy of wage restraint in Italy. An Interministerial Committee on Prices (CIP), established under a law of 1944, still exists and has been used to regulate prices in certain distributive areas (especially public utilities) and services. However, it bases its regulations on the costs of marginal firms and seems to act as a kind of resale price maintenance institution. In this

[11] See the wage equation in footnote 7.

respect, the Italians apparently lack the kind of price mechanisms which the French deployed on past occasions, with some apparent success.

Political instability and economic resilience.

The last quarter of 1969 lived up to its advance billing as "the hot autumn" as a wave of strikes affected more than a million workers, and wage increases were granted which raised manufacturing labor costs by 16 per cent and more in 1970. This most recent explosion occurred against a background of declining unemployment and declining current surplus in the balance of payments, but when both the balance and unemployment (at 3.4 per cent of the work force) were still quite high and the rate of price inflation was quite moderate.[12] It was thus a clear example of "premature inflation." Much of this increase was offset by rising productivity, inflation abroad, and more moderate increases in the prices of imported raw materials.[13] Yet the granting of such large wage increases posed a serious risk of inflation or unemployment. Nevertheless the unions, although not unmindful of these hazards, sought them; and neither the large companies nor the bank were disposed to deny them.

The reason is that Italians, with a deep political crisis on their hands, feared that radical students and others on the New Left threatened to influence younger workers (especially recent migrants from the South) and that an Italian version of the 1968 near-revolution in France was a distinct possibility. Under the circumstances, a wage explosion without social upheaval was preferable to a wage explosion with social upheaval. It was for this reason that the union federations cooperated closely (if

[12] OECD Economic Surveys, *Italy,* July 1970, pp. 43–44.
[13] *The Economist,* March 14, 1970, p. vii.

sometimes warily) with one another, that the established union leadership sought to consult the preferences of the members before the formulation of bargaining demands, and that they included prominently among the latter the demand for bargaining at the plant level (as a means of absorbing the shop stewards into the union movement). And it is for this reason that employers – especially those in large-scale enterprises – granted these demands. In a society where the official institutions were extremely weak, the employers wished to maintain the union establishment as it, too, came under attack from the membership. They needed, as one of them put it, someone to bargain with. Nor were economic policy makers disposed to contribute to the strain on the centralized institutional fabric of the labor movement which the jawbone approach would have predictably imposed. The *ex post* approach of deflation and more unemployment was implicitly – and in some cases, explicitly – preferred to the *ex ante* approach of incomes policy.

SUMMARY

In Italy, interest in an incomes policy was a byproduct of a wage explosion of uncertain origin and subsequent balance-of-payments deficits in the early 1960's, rather than of a history of persistent conflict between growth of incomes and goals of economic policy. However, there are indications that the effectiveness of monetary policy has been diminishing and that the forms of institutional behavior which have induced conflict among objectives in other countries merely developed later in Italy. Hence the difficulties which have impelled other countries to adopt incomes policies may be more evident in the future.

The government objective was to restrain incomes by imbedding a wage policy within the 1966–1970 development plan. In the event, however, the discussion of incomes policy within the plan document was quite general and included neither a wage guideline nor a price guideline. The wage guideline was omitted because the parties it was intended to restrain did not agree with planning, on largely ideological grounds. Moreover, there were indications that the policy would not only be ignored by unions, but would be a positive irritant to the increasingly militant rank and file groups, thereby inducing further social unrest. The public-sector industries were unwilling to administer a guideline that would interfere with their attempts to modernize industrial relations practices; moreover, they favored a structural theory of recent Italian inflation. Furthermore, the omission of a price guideline presumably would have resulted in the erosion of any wage policy, in the light of econometric evidence of the exceedingly strong role of price movements in aggregate wage determination. Finally, the wave of strikes, both wildcat and official, in 1969-1970 and the continuing political disequilibrium virtually precluded the introduction of incomes policy in Italy.

CONCLUSIONS AND PROSPECTS

Incomes policy, to generalize from the experience of the countries studied in this account, has not been very successful. The gravity of the problem to which incomes policy is addressed and the lack of satisfactory alternative solutions have combined to give the policy a good run for its money—and may well ensure return engagements. Yet the accumulation of experience in the countries studied in this account suggest that in none of the variations so far turned up has incomes policy succeeded in its fundamental objective, as stated, of making full employment consistent with a reasonable degree of price stability.

It may be that its sights had been set too high; had less been expected of the policy, it might have performed more effectively. The record suggests that it might operate most efficiently in the short run under conditions of excess supply. Then it might help to hold down wage and price increases in an economy short of full employment. It would do so primarily by inducing employers to resist union demands more firmly, but some self-restraint by unions and managers would also be required, especially if the slack periods were associated with rising prices and lagging wages. (The Prices and Incomes Commission of Canada abandoned its voluntary guidelines at the end of 1970 when the employers withdrew support of the price guides. Their decision, in turn, was attributed to refusal by the unions to accept a 6 per cent target for wage increases.)

However, in Europe, where unemployment rates have prevailed at considerably lower levels than in the United States, incomes policy had been assigned a more ambitious role. The modest short-run assignment would have signified acceptance of recurrent spells of relatively high unemployment and slack; and policy effectiveness at this level would not have spelled success. Therefore, instead of regarding incomes policy as an aid in periodically regaining full employment, they regarded it as an aid in maintaining a steady state of full employment. This implied a long-term, continuing role for incomes policy and necessarily made its effectiveness in restraining wages and prices more dependent on inducing unions and enterprises to curb their appetites rather than inducing employers to resist union demands.

Nevertheless, conditions determining the effectiveness of such a steady-state policy—which would include the relative importance of external and domestic economic objectives, the distribution of income, the degree to which labor and employer organizations are centralized, the degree of legal enforcement accorded to incomes policy, and the public tolerance of industrial stoppages and worker unrest—obviously help to determine the effectiveness of short-term incomes policy as well. Drawing on the experience of our seven countries, this chapter attempts a fresh evaluation of such conditions and of some rather widely held propositions concerning the effectiveness of policies to promote wage and price restraint.

A REAPPRAISAL OF OBJECTIVES?

The importance of the currency crisis.

Incomes policies have been designed to make a contribution to three major objectives: domestic price stability, balance-of-payments equilibrium, and a high rate of economic growth. In addition, they frequently have been designed to help redistribute income in favor of the employed poor. Among these goals, equilibrium in the balance of payments has traditionally been assigned the highest priority, at least in those countries whose experience we have examined in this study. This assignment reflects a tendency to value domestic price restraint more for its contribution to external balance than in its own right.[1]

Two consequences flowed from this ordering of priorities. First, insofar as a country did not require absolute price stability to achieve stability in its balance of payments, the task of incomes policy was made lighter. In the Netherlands, proponents of incomes policy claim that it was effective in depressing the levels of costs and prices relative to those of the country's international competitors, thereby contributing to equilibrium in the balance of payments, although the policy may not have been very effective in maintaining price stability at home. (The Scandinavian model of "imported inflation" seeks to explain how balance-of-payments equilibrium could coexist with domestic price inflation in small open economies. It offers the hypothesis that wage increases originate in the competitive foreign-trade sectors, where they are largely absorbed by relatively fast-growing productivity, but that they spread into the "sheltered" and more slowly growing sectors, where they force up prices.)

[1] R. A. Gordon, *The Goal of Full Employment* (New York: Wiley, 1967), p. 29.

Moreover, the existence of a balance-of-payments crisis, or even a clearly perceived threat of such an occurrence, has acted as a most effective stimulus to the adoption and support of incomes policy. In the absence of a currency crisis unionists might be unaware of the existence of a trade-off between inflation and unemployment, or else they might have good political reason to believe that inflationary wage increases need not entail deflationary consequences. But they have learned from hard experience that a currency crisis is most likely to be associated with increased unemployment, for then the authorities' area of discretion is severely circumscribed. Moreover, unionists are more likely to accept restraint with good grace under such circumstances. The currency crisis thus furnishes one example of the civilizing influence of common adversity on communal behavior. Wartime of course provides the leading case in point; indeed the response of the Dutch to the German occupation furnished the basis for the most determined attempts by unions and employers to forge an effective incomes policy. This does not mean that common adversity invariably generated incomes policies—the Swedes resisted the temptation in the late 1960's—but it could almost be regarded as a necessary condition thereof in the countries included in this study.

But developments in the sixties, and even before, might have reduced somewhat the relative importance of balance-of-payments considerations as both policy objective and stimulus. In the first place, it became apparent that the capacity of incomes policy to contribute to external balance was quite limited. While the policy might help to tide an overheated economy over a transitional period of difficulty (as in Italy), it was clearly not up to the task of eliminating a "fundamental disequilibrium" in a country's balance of payments. British experience under the Wilson government made it evident that incomes policy could provide no alternative to currency devaluation.

Secondly, the relative effectiveness of the actual or anticipated currency crisis as a stimulus to the implementation of incomes policy might have undergone some weakening, although this is by no means clear. The reactions against union leadership in the Netherlands in 1955–1957 and in Britain a decade later showed that even the existence of emergency conditions could not render cooperative labor leaders immune from rank-and-file criticism. The Dutch planners, as we have noted, expressed concern over what they regarded as public indifference to "our competitive position." However, there did not appear to be much cause for anxiety in most countries, since, at the beginning of the seventies, competitive positions still reflected the equilibrating influence of a series of currency adjustments.

Price inflation as stimulus.

On the other hand, this apparent relative stability in international economic relationships was accompanied by an international bout of wage-price inflation. Thus, if the latter proves influential in reviving incomes policy, it could mean that price inflation is coming to the fore as a policy objective in its own right. (The support given to incomes policy by such international agencies as the Organisation for Economic Co-operation and Development and the International Monetary Fund has not been confined to prescriptions for debtor countries; the OECD has long viewed the policy as an instrument to promote the objective of economic growth by restraining consumption, and the IMF and the central bankers have been traditionally haunted by the spectre of global inflation.)

Dissatisfaction with domestic price increases has been more influential than uneasiness over the balance of payments in inducing Dutch unions and businessmen to revive the cooperative working relationships which had underpinned their quest for an effective and durable incomes policy in the past. It has also played a major role in persuading the Swedes, those determined opponents of formal incomes policy, to introduce price controls in 1970. Should new incomes policies arise on this new foundation, the experiments would be watched with considerable interest in the United States. For the Kennedy *Guideposts,* although initiated during a period of price stability and at a time when policy makers were indeed concerned about the balance of payments, were primarily aimed at preventing inflation from emerging and aborting the recovery which the administration's expansionist policies were designed to promote.

But what would the revival of incomes policy in response to domestic inflation signify? In the first place, it would reflect the view that inflation in contemporary society is caused by private power as well as—or rather, in conjunction with—official policy. The fact that inflation was so frequently associated with excess demand and low unemployment has not demolished the view that cost-push forces have contributed to the inflationary process, even in countries where the conventional institutional generators of cost-push have been regarded as notoriously weak. For wage inflation has also occurred when profits were being squeezed (Italy in the early sixties, West Germany between the early fifties and the early sixties, Sweden after the mid-sixties) and when unemployment was relatively high (wage drift in Denmark, the wage explosions near the end of the decade in France, Italy, and the United Kingdom). Cost-of-living indexation in countries with such disparate institutional frameworks as Italy and Denmark also created some presumption of cost-push influences, as did econometric evidence of apparently high sensitivity of wages to prior increases in prices in most of the countries studied.

Secondly, average wage behavior in Italy, France, and West Germany was not well explained by reference to unemployment. This doubtless reflects data deficiencies as well as the unsuitability of unemployment as a proxy for "demand-pull" influences, especially in Germany. But it may also suggest that wage-setting in economies which are subject to considerable oligopolistic influences, and, in Italy and France, to the influence of politically oriented labor movements might be too complex a process to yield to conventional categorization. What seems widely agreed is that, although the mix of political and direct economic pressures exerted by the various labor movements may vary widely, the totality of their social influence is often sufficiently great to impose restraint on economic policy and performance. It is regarded as sufficient to withhold a significant degree of autonomy from the monetary and fiscal authorities.

The popularity of incomes policy also reflects the belief that, whether the unions are "blamed" for a particular bout of inflation or not (as in the Swedish version of the Aukrust model), they are strong enough to hold down the growth of money incomes. This has been the basis of much of the advocacy of incomes policy, including the unofficial and privately administered Swedish variety as well as the more formal, governmentally sponsored policy found elsewhere. It reflects what, in discussing Dutch experience, we referred to as quasi government: that social problems which do not yield to competitive pressures arising from individual activity should be tackled, not by the state alone, but by "interest group activities" which may have caused them in the first place. Thus a revival of incomes policy might testify to growing public impatience with inflation and to the belief that private-interest groups would be able, if made willing, to contribute significantly to price stability.

But a revival could not reflect satisfaction with past performance. Not that incomes policies were totally ineffective, if one goes by econometric attempts to approximate what would have happened in their absence. Wages sometimes seemed to rise less rapidly than underlying "structural" conditions would have led one to expect (even in France, Italy, and Germany); and sometimes prices seemed to rise less relative to wages than might have been expected. However, as indicated at the outset, periods of apparent effectiveness were typically short-lived; they were frequently followed by wage or price explosions which sometimes blew up the policies themselves. Thus the policy at best seems to have been gaited for a short sprint rather than a long race, which suggests that it was better suited to deal with short-run emergencies like transient balance-of-payments disequilibria than with persistent inflationary forces. Moreover, the evidence strongly suggests that the policies were not effective in containing wage drift—whether "compensatory," and primarily initiated by employers seeking to overcome labor shortages, or "imitative" and due to "push" exerted by dissatisfied local employees. Taken together, these two pervasive limitations on the policy's effectiveness in curbing incomes and prices suggest, first, that powerful private interest groups were not always willing and able to restrain themselves in the public interest; and, second, that, when they did cooperate, their efforts could be nullified by—and could even induce—"irresponsible" wage and price behavior outside their orbits of influence.

EDUCATION, PERSUASION, AND THE DISTRIBUTION OF INCOME

The effectiveness of incomes policy, at least under conditions of excess demand, depends importantly upon its ability to restrain the behavior of unions. That capacity is in turn a function of both the policy's persuasiveness and the coercive power brought to bear in its support, the intention being to minimize the degree of compulsion required at any given level of effectiveness. And behind persuasiveness, so the theory goes, lies education—education about the role played by excessive wage increases in forcing the community to choose between inflation and unemployment; education about the limited ability of unionism to force a redistribution of income; education about the need to choose between income redistribution and economic growth; and education about the apparent incompatibility between what the British have termed "free-for-all" bargaining and the objective of a more egalitarian distribution of wage (as well as total) income, which many labor movements have long espoused.

Whether the policy engine could be fueled by persuasion and education alone—without the additive of governmental sanction—is a moot point; but it seems to have been generally agreed that persuasion, hence education, is an indispensable and a major ingredient. Therefore there has been some disposition to regard the disappointing performances of incomes policy as evidence of failed experiments in adult education. Hence the gloomy assessment of the British Prices and Incomes Board at the end of the decade: "The need to learn the lessons of economic choice is as urgent as ever it was."

Yet the main lesson to be learned is not that organized groups are slow to appreciate the wider consequences of their actions, for, true as that may be, evidence of such sophistication among unionists was not lacking in the 1960's. Rather the main lesson is that enlightenment need not entail self-restraint, or at least it need not entail sufficient self-restraint to reasonably satisfy the requirements of price stability. What until recently distinguished the German unionists from their colleagues in Italy and Scandinavia was not greater economic sophistication, but greater inhibition.

Examination of the record yields various reasons for the frequent failure of educational effectiveness to be concerned with effective wage restraint. At the heart of all, save the last, lies disagreement between one or more of the "social partners" and the authorities about the policy's potential impact on the distribution of income. Of course, no disagreement would occur if two conditions obtain: (a) the private-interest groups are not made especially unhappy by the existing distribution of income; and (b) the introduction of an incomes policy would not change either that income distribution or the state of emotions which that distribution has been generating. Under such conditions, publication of a set of quantified guidelines could well prove effective. By removing inflationary expectations it could put an end to what might be regarded as *defensive* inflationary behavior, whereby each group seeks primarily to maintain its share of the national income. If, however, both conditions do not obtain, the policy may find itself in trouble.

To begin with, the policy itself might, intentionally

of inadvertently, result in an adverse redistribution of income, from the viewpoint of the union interest. It may do so deliberately when the object is to cope with a balance-of-payments emergency by a freeze on wages or prices or both. Even if prices are frozen as effectively as wages, increasing productivity would tend to redistribute income in favor of profits. This might facilitate an "export-led upswing," but conceivably at the expense of subsequent promotion of long-term price stability through wage restraint. For if a long-term productivity-based policy were tacked on to the end of a limited-duration freeze, the unions would be denied an opportunity to recoup the once-for-all loss which they had incurred during the "emergency."

An incomes policy might even be designed to secure a permanent reduction in the actual or potential share of labor income in order to promote a higher rate of economic growth. Such a policy might be defended on the grounds that it would ultimately make possible a higher rate of growth of labor income; but it might prove difficult to persuade union representatives to sanction this type of investment in the future. Thus French unions began to attack the official growth targets as unduly restrictive of social-assistance payments. It is not unreasonable to expect lower-income groups to prefer the bird in the hand.

In addition, most incomes policies have sought to effect a redistribution of labor income itself, by making provision for higher rates of wage increase for workers with very low pay. European labor movements, especially in Scandinavia and the United Kingdom, have espoused egalitarian wage philosophies; and it was hoped that their inability to implement egalitarianism under laissez-faire conditions might predispose them in favor of incomes policy. Now this redistributive aspect of incomes policy has indeed attracted support within the ranks of the trade unionists; but the intensity of such support seems to vary inversely with distance from the grass roots and, to some extent (especially when white-collar unionists are added in), with level of income. This is not to deny a union commitment to the diversion of a larger share of the national income to the low-paid. But one thing seems clear: unionists have not regarded a redistribution of wage income in favor of the low-paid as compensation for redistribution away from wage income in the interest of economic growth (and hence profits).

Incomes policy might also be a source of income redistribution which is undesired by the policy maker as well as the trade unionist. Thus it is conducive to a shift against institutionally or collectively determined incomes and in favor of more atomistically or of residually determined incomes. The latter include both locally determined wage drift and profits (especially in the form of retained earnings). (The president of the Board of Chairmen of the Danish Economic Council, after staking out a modest but constructive role for an incomes policy operated "by persuasion," observed: "The trouble is that you can't really promise anything as to profits.")[2]

Now if incomes policy could restrain administered prices and wages, it should not be reproached, as it has been, for failing to restrain the more competitively determined wages and prices as well. It is designed to cope only with "push" inflation; and if it accomplished only this objective it would serve the interests of both price stability and economic efficiency. However, if those

[2] *On Incomes Policy: Papers and Proceedings from a Conference in Honour of Erik Lundberg* (Stockholm: The Industrial Council for Social and Economic Studies, 1969), p. 45.

wages and prices beyond the reach of incomes policy cannot be restrained by other means—as they cannot under conditions of excess demand—the effectiveness of the policy within its own proper domain is bound to be severely limited. This is a major reason why the range within which incomes policy can be substituted for fiscal-monetary restraint is limited.

The publication of an official, quantified norm, guidepost, or target might itself result in a redistribution of income against wages. This could result if the wage norm emerges from conservatively biased forecasts. Thus if money wage rates were constrained to rise less rapidly than productivity rose in fact (and if compensatory drift did not make up the difference), unit labor costs would fall. If prices did not follow unit labor costs downward, profits would rise more rapidly than wages. British, Dutch, and Swedish union spokesmen have charged that government forecasts and official norms are in fact biased conservatively; and such instances of underprediction as occurred in the Federal Republic in 1961 and the Netherlands in 1963 lend substance to the general charge. Although it does not imply intent to short-change the wage earners, forecasting bias nevertheless has served to undermine confidence in the norm. (It might be maintained that this source of distrust could be eliminated by basing current wage norms on past trends, rather than prospective movements, in productivity, in the manner of the *U.S. Guideposts.* This should alleviate the problem, but some difficulties would remain. First, guideposts based on trend productivity might lack versatility and flexibility; they might not readily be adapted to cope with balance-of-payments emergencies or, for that matter, to produce price stability, year in and year out. Second, there would still be considerable scope for argument over what the "correct" trend productivity figure should be; witness the vigorous "bargaining" over productivity data that occurred in the Netherlands between 1959 and 1963.)

Nor would an incomes policy which could reasonably be expected to leave the distribution of income unchanged ensure union acceptance. If the unions happen to be actively dissatisfied with that distribution, their *offensive* behavior could be reflected in inflation. (The inflation would reflect the fact that the sum of the claims of the various social partners, organized and otherwise, exceeds the total national income at constant prices.) Under such circumstances, attempts to secure an economic peace treaty, or social contract, based on acceptance of the existing distribution of income have not proved notably successful. The failures of formal and public *concertation* in France and Denmark bear witness to the limitations of *cohérence* when persuasion requires more than education. Indeed, the demands by the CFDT in France and the LO in Denmark for more and more statistical information on the distribution of income and assets both among persons and within the firm shows how educational materials can be converted into tools of advocacy. When disagreement about the distribution of income is elevated to the status of ideological imperative, increased sophistication concerning the trade-off between inflation and unemployment might produce a negative incomes policy. This allegedly occurred in Italy where the Communist-led CGIL justified intemperate wage demands precisely because of their presumptively destabilizing effect on the capitalist economic order.

Conversely, one might almost go so far as to say that an attempt to obtain restraint through *concertation* can be counted on to provoke disagreement over the distribution of income. It can awaken sleeping dogs. In Denmark, it has been suggested, *concertation* made it more difficult for the union movement to continue to exercise even as much restraint as it had done previously, in an unofficial and rather unpublicized way. The issuance of a norm could also exert a similar perverse effect. No union leader worth his salt could afford to pass up the opportunity to exceed an official guidepost if he wanted to justify his existence to the dues payers—especially if he believed that other union leaders would have to earn their salt the same way, or that shop stewards and employers would step up the pace of drift. Thus the Dutch stopped publishing wage targets in 1967, claiming that they had served as minimum targets, rather than as maxima. In Denmark, a string of highly similar norms (based largely on productivity) led to suggestions that publication be ceased, for the unions could not be placed in a position (at least in a public position) of acting like a rubber stamp. Swedish union spokesmen rejected a suggestion that contractually negotiated wage incomes be determined as a statistical residual largely for the same reason. Perhaps the way out is to explore the potentialities of a no-norm policy.

THE RECENT TREND IN INCOME DISTRIBUTIONS

Thus far we have seen that there is no particular reason why unions should cooperate with a policy which itself tended, intentionally or otherwise, to redistribute income away from the bulk of its membership. To withhold cooperation would prevent such an undesired redistribution. But are there equal grounds for expecting that union movements would not cooperate with a policy which could be counted on not to affect the distribution of income adversely from their viewpoint? True, as we have argued, the unionists might be dissatisfied with the existing distribution of income, but what could they do about it anyway? Could they not be made to recognize that, (a) instead of effecting the desired redistribution, pushing up wages simply generates price inflation, which in turn (b) forces the authorities to take countermeasures resulting in unemployment and income loss instead of full employment and faster growth? And might not the latter consideration outweigh the strong institutional liabilities incurred in cooperation, so that acceptance of even a badly regarded distribution under conditions of restraint would be preferable to acceptance of that distribution with deflation?

REGRESSIONS OF LABOR'S SHARE IN NATIONAL INCOME
(Annual data, 1957–1967; t statistics in parentheses)

	Regression Number	Constant	Unemployment Rate	Time	R^2	Durbin-Watson Statistic
Denmark	(1)	52.49 (46.05)	.36 (2.97)	.95 (9.61)	.959	2.309
France	(2)	44.05 (29.59)	.565 (.889)	.71 (8.07)	.919	1.674
Germany	(3)	51.85 (82.02)	−.05 (.27)	.76 (11.89)	.967	1.143
Italy	(4)	53.75 (20.80)	−.41 (1.12)	.72 (3.69)	.858	.949
Netherlands	(5)	46.93 (42.63)	−.45 (.74)	.58 (5.80)	.822	1.129
Sweden	(6)	58.25 (37.99)	−.15 (.20)	.70 (7.39)	.915	1.776
United Kingdom	(7)	69.05 (51.25)	−.75 (1.69)	.24 (5.07)	.776	1.494
United States	(8)	63.95 (60.46)	.12 (.74)	.04 (.70)	.099	2.051

SOURCE: OECD, *National Accounts of OECD Countries* (Paris: 1968, 1969); ILO, *Yearbook of Labour Statistics, 1969* (Geneva: 1969).

The general answer to the first two questions is that logic need not prevail among those who find its message unpalatable—and that it is virtually certain not to carry the day when it gives the appearance of flying in the face of evidence. The evidence in this instance consists of pronounced upward movements in the share of wages and salaries in the national incomes in the seven countries, in the decade beginning in 1957. After allowing for variations in unemployment, significant trends are shown in the regression equations in the table, "Regressions of Labor's Share in National Income." In Britain, where the labor share was initially high, the average annual rate of increase was lowest, but significant, at .24 percentage points. Elsewhere, the trend values ranged from .58 of a point in the Netherlands to .95 in Denmark. These findings are consistent with the operation of any number of causal factors, possibly including a postwar tightening of the labor supply available to industrialized countries on the Continent and also a shift of the working population out of low-income sectors such as agriculture. They might or might not reflect the cumulative effects of labor movement pressures. But that is beside the point. A labor movement cannot be expected to lend protracted support to any policy which contemplates the arresting – let alone the reversal – of such an ongoing process. In terms of our discussion, the existence of a trend in favor of wages and salaries might well be regarded as evidence of labor's dissatisfaction with the distribution of income at any given point in time. No such trend exists in the United States data. Therefore, on this count alone, one might expect to encounter less union resistance in the United States to a policy which contemplates an unchanged distribution of income.

FRIENDLY PERSUASION AND EXPECTED LOSS

But if the rate of inflation associated with rising labor shares is excessive, might not labor still be better off by accepting an incomes policy than by suffering the consequences of deflation?

The answer to this question is likely to depend on the economic vantage point of the respondent. Let us consider the two extremes. At the level of the central federation, the question might be answered in the affirmative. Top-level decision makers in the labor movement might accept the formulation of the official policy maker—although they seem somewhat less unwilling to learn their economics from laborite or socialist ministers than from liberals or conservatives. (The rejection of "capitalistic" planning by Communist-led federations in Italy and France is the most obvious illustration of this point.) At ground level, however, the individual unionist might reply in the negative. He has good reason to believe that, in the event of a deflation of the postwar stop-go-stop variety, the probability that he will lose his job is low indeed; in fact it might be zero—especially if he is a senior employee or if there are substantial pockets of structural unemployment elsewhere in the economy. Thus the typical individual might be confronted with a choice quite different from that posed in the preceding paragraph. His is the choice between a low probability of income loss through unemployment in the event of deflation and a rather high probability of loss of, at least potential, income under a policy of wage restraint. This, in discussing the apparently attenuated fear of unemployment in Britain and the effect of structural unemployment in Denmark, we referred to on page 36 as the theory of expected loss. It implies that the failure of individuals to respond to a plea for wage restraint in the public interest may not reflect failure to appreciate the nature of the trade-off between wage-price movements and unemployment in the aggregate. The representative member might be quite as sophisticated as his leader and yet pass a negative verdict on incomes policy. And of course the position held by a significant proportion of the membership will in time influence the response of the central leadership.

On the other hand, the individual's attitude is influenced by the policies and the powers of the central federation itself. The individual's position depends, as we know, on the probability that money-wage increases foregone under incomes policy will be translated into lower relative or even actual real income than he could have obtained under a regime of laissez-faire. Now this probability is determined in part by how many other individuals, in other unions, would comply with the policy if he did. And the extent of compliance depends in part on the degree of influence and power possessed by the central federation.

UNION STRUCTURE AND INSTITUTIONAL CHANGE

Thus it is understandable that a highly centralized trade-union movement should have been regarded in many quarters as the *sine qua non* for an effective incomes policy. In fact, when a powerful central organization represents a substantial proportion of a country's work force, it might have to be guided by consideration of the wider ramifications of its wage policy whether or not (as in Sweden) a governmental incomes policy is in effect. ("In Sweden, there has been centralized bargaining since 1956," wrote the economic adviser to the Swedish Employers' Confederation. "That means, essentially, that we have practised a national policy as far as wage and salary incomes are concerned.")[3]

[3] K. O. Faxén, "Incomes Policy in Sweden: Problems and Developments," *British Journal of Industrial Relations,* November 1964, p. 340.

Conversely, it has been frequently argued that the prior existence of a weak central federation, as in the United States or Britain, is enough to seal the fate of any incomes policy at the outset. But the educational function of incomes policy should result in institutional change, where appropriate, although this need not always require a change in formal structures. Thus the Dutch were able to mount an apparently effective incomes policy, although their workers were organized into three separate union movements and although bargaining was conducted at industry level by formally autonomous national unions. Incomes policy in the Netherlands helped to generate *de facto* central bargaining despite these unpromising initial structural conditions. On the other hand, it failed to produce the same result in Britain, despite the efforts of the top leadership to induce the affiliates to cede some authority over wage determination to the Trades Union Congress. The leaders argued that, the greater the self-restraint exercised by the labor movement, the less would be the need for society to impose restraint upon it. Their ideal was the Swedish substitute for official incomes policy, but they sought to make use of an official policy to secure that ideal. Their failure underscored the inability of incomes policy at the time to persuade people into self-reform.

Moreover, even in Sweden—and *a fortiori* elsewhere—the limitations on private power were too great to make the theory of expected loss work decisively on the side of restraint. The central labor federation's effective span of control is sharply limited with respect to both its vertical and horizontal dimensions. The vertical limitation consists of the lack (certainly by American standards) of grass roots: European unions typically do not reach down to the plant level where shop stewards, works councils, and employers operate beyond their control. This does not imply that the central federation is wholly without influence; in France and Italy, where the anarchistic tradition is still strong, the top federations can get people to walk off the job, although they might not be successful in getting them to pay dues. But the decline in the popularity of socialist ideology and the spirit of working class solidarity and egalitarianism which generated that ideology has clearly limited the influence of the central federation within the trade-union movement. The average wage earner would not be impulsively moved by appeals based either on party loyalty or on the welfare of his less fortunate brethren.

The result was locally generated wage drift which sometimes "compensated" for movements in centrally negotiated wage rates. Thus drift could offset restraint at higher levels; it could even tend to erode central authority within the union movement; and, as some Dutch union leaders fear, it could contribute to a decline in the popularity of unionism itself, especially among the new generation of workers. Wildcat strikes, which had long been a way of British life, gave dramatic evidence of union weakness at the grass roots in 1968–1969, when they spread from France into Italy, thence to the Federal Republic of Germany, and even into Sweden. These demonstrations cannot be laid at the door of incomes policy, but they served notice that the central labor federation would be a frailer reed for policy to lean on in the future than it had been in the past.

The horizontal limitations on the federation's zone of influence further reduce its effectiveness as an instrument of policy. We implicitly alluded to this in discussing the tendency of incomes policy to be selectively effective, which reflects the fact that the restraining influence of the central federation might not extend far beyond the population of union members. Indeed, it may not go that far.

Associations of salaried employees, whether affiliated with the central organization (as in Britain) or with separate federations (as in Sweden) have proved particularly reluctant to subscribe to policies of restraint. White-collar employees, many of whom work for the government and few of whom are paid under incentive systems, have less opportunity to generate "drift"; and their incomes may suffer relative reduction under the combined effect of inflation and progressive tax structures.

Moreover, the inability of the blue-collar organizations to lead these and other income groups in restraint tended to reduce the central federation's "vertical" authority within its own blue-collar jurisdictions, and thus its willingness to support official policy. Sweden furnishes an example of a country whose strongly centralized labor federation has come under both external and internal challenge. The former has been led by a federation of high-echelon salaried employees and professionals; evidence of the latter has taken the form of wage drift and wildcat strikes, some of which have been directed against the central union negotiators as well as against the employers. Thus incomes policy, designed to make possible a higher rate of economic growth and based to some extent on the power of centralized institutional structures, can contribute to decentralizing influences and even to growth-retarding industrial unrest.

ENFORCEMENT, PERSUASION, AND INDUSTRIAL PEACE

In view of the limitations of quasi government in inducing wage restraint, it is not surprising that when countries took their incomes policies seriously they frequently decided to spike the brew with something stronger than exhortation, education, and even economic planning. Three favorite extra ingredients were: direct restraint of the public sector, legal sanctions, and price controls. It should be noted, however, that these official measures were not designed to displace quasi government; in fact, it was hoped that they would facilitate cooperation by organized labor and management. They could also implement wage restraint policy in more direct ways, of course, but such benefits would have to be weighed against any costs they might incur in reducing, rather than raising, the level of voluntary cooperation. And when such policies were carried to the point of generating negative cooperation—in the form of strikes and other manifestations of unrest—the authorities had to balance the social goals of minimizing unemployment and maximizing price stability with the social goal of maximizing industrial peace.

The public sector.

The urge to impose wage restraint on the government sector could almost be regarded as instinctive, even among conservative governments which do not favor incomes policy in principle. For the government presumably has some discretion as an employer and the magnitude of the public payroll can enter rather directly into the calculations of the fiscal and monetary authorities. And apart from its direct impact on the level of costs and demand, restraint imposed on public wages and salaries should, according to one theory, induce voluntary restraint in the private sector. This assumes that one determinant of the level of private restraint is the maintenance of the existing relationship between labor incomes in the two sectors. Thus in 1963 the Danish authorities hoped that severe restraints on the salaries of civil servants would help to induce the LO to accept a 3 per cent wage norm, since the latter would no longer have to anticipate that the government employees might subsequently be able to improve on the private settlements.

But this theory ignores the traditional mechanism by which the public-private wage relationship is in fact determined: the private sector usually sets the pace and the government sector, invoking the principle of "comparability," follows to restore the relationship. What the policy under consideration contemplates, therefore, is a reversal of roles. But the mere promise of maintenance of wage relativities has not been too successful in inducing private wage setters to surrender their leadership. The determination not to be left behind does not, unfortunately, imply unwillingness to step out in front. Thus the private sector might simply not respond to a standstill in the public sector; this occurred during a British "pay pause" in 1962. As a result, pressure builds up for a quantum jump in lagging public wages and salaries; thus we noted that, during the French wage explosion of 1968, the greatest increases tended to be concentrated among groups of public employees whose wages had previously been subject to the most determined governmental restraint. And, finally, a big catch-up increase in public wages, which can of course be reflected in the price indices, help to touch off a new round of increases in the private sector. Therefore, the Dutch, notwithstanding their commitment to incomes policy, have refrained from using the public sector as either a cutting edge or a rearguard.

The policy rests on one other questionable assumption. It is assumed that the government as an employer can be made more resistant to wage demands than private employers. There are two reasons for doubting this. In the first place, services rendered by public employees are often regarded as highly essential to the community. Therefore, the government might find it difficult to take strikes; it is probably no easier for a British or French government to endure a strike on a nationalized railroad than for an American government to endure a strike on a privately owned railroad. Indeed (and this is the second reason), the political pressure on the government for maintaining or for resumption of operations in an enterprise might well be greater if that enterprise is run by the government than if it is privately owned and operated.

Legal sanctions and industrial peace.

In most countries, at one time or another, governments have intervened directly to restrain wages in the private sector as well as in the public sector. In addition to the publication of guidelines, such intervention has taken various forms. The guidelines themselves might be legislated, especially when a "freeze" was called for (as in the case of Denmark in 1963 or Britain in 1966–1967). A special agency would usually be established to interpret the guidelines and apply them in specific instances. It might be confined to post mortems, or it might be empowered to do pre-audits—requiring advance notice of all intended wage (or price) increases and even inspecting the firm's books. It might be able to delay enactment of such changes until it had completed its examination, and it might even be permitted to nullify contracts which it had found excessive. Finally, failure to comply with the policy might entail legal sanctions (as in the prohibitions against negotiating or paying "black wages" in the Netherlands).

But legal intervention or compulsion has always been regarded as supplementary to or supportive of voluntary acceptance. Two arguments were advanced in favor of a mandatory wage-price freeze in Britain in the summer of 1966. The first was the rogue-elephant theory, which was invoked in reply to the argument that legal restraints are bound to be ineffective in the absence of popular support of a policy and that, given popular support, legal restraints were not necessary. In rebuttal it was urged that popular support can be maintained only if the occasional rogue elephant is effectively disciplined; for this purpose legislation is both effective and necessary to establish the appropriate level of expectations. A second argument went further. It was claimed that the passage of legislation would itself help to create the degree of popular acceptance necessary to make the policy enforceable: up to a point, respect for the law could substitute for persuasion on the merits. Of course, it could be objected (especially on this side of the Atlantic, but abroad as well) that this relationship could hold in reverse: unpopular legislation helps to undermine respect for the law. It could also be argued that it is precisely the rogue elephant who tests and defines the level of liberty in a community. But these points could be taken simply as helpful in defining the tolerable limits of mandated restraint. The fact that experiments along these lines were conducted in Britain, Denmark, and the Netherlands without noticeable impairment to their standing as centers of civil liberty suggests that tolerable limits were not in fact exceeded. This is not to imply that these experiments were undertaken with alacrity; on the contrary, the more extensive restraints were accepted only as emergency measures. (Thus the Dutch NVV, while accepting the need for a compulsory freeze in times of emergency, rejected detailed intervention in collective bargaining as practiced by the Board of Mediators.)

But a more valid objection to legal restraints, it seems

to us, is that, within the democratically permissible limits to which they have been held, and in the economic climate to which they have been subjected, they have not proved sufficiently effective. In Britain at least the evidence suggests that (with the exception of an early postwar "voluntary" freeze) incomes policy proved most effective when it was reinforced by legal authority of one form or another; but even there, as elsewhere, the reinforced policy was effective for only limited time and it was likely to be either followed—or terminated—by "explosions." We have thus suggested that the cost of short-term freezing runs in terms of long-run moderation. If so, it appears that the ability of legal authority to persuade has thus far proved quite limited—at least under prevailing conditions of demand.

One reason why governmental fiat and sanction were pushed neither beyond democratically permissible limits nor up to the limits of long-term effectiveness is that the government of the day was reluctant to incur the levels of industrial unrest which more stringent sanctions and attempts at enforcement could arouse. In the Netherlands, the government on more than one occasion felt it impossible to exercise its legal authority. In Britain, incomes policy was subordinated to industrial peace by effectively subordinating the independent National Board for Prices and Incomes to the Department of Employment and Productivity (formerly Ministry of Labour). In Denmark, state arbitrators (mediators) are authorized to make their own recommendations; but concern lest they impair their future credibility with the private parties has not made it advisable for them to overburden their recommendation for dispute settlement with considerations of broader economic implications.

On the other hand, some econometric studies suggest that the frequency of strikes varies inversely with both the rate of change of real wages—that is, of money wages relative to prices—and the rate of unemployment.[4] Moreover, these studies show that a decline in the rate of increase in money wages is more likely to provoke stoppages than an accelerated price increase. This suggests that, if an incomes policy bears down more heavily on money wages than on prices and thereby slows down the growth of real wages, it is likely to generate more strikes—whether or not it is enforced by legal sanctions.[5] Hence the causal agent may be the potential effectiveness of the policy as well as the instrument of its enforcement. In either event the policy maker is likely to feel inhibited. Thus industrial peace again emerges as a social objective in its own right, constraining policies designed to minimize both unemployment and inflation.

Price restraint.

Policies aimed directly at restraining price behavior were adopted in all countries except Italy and Germany. However, in the absence of restraint on labor costs, price controls would tend to squeeze profits and thus either to abort an upswing or, at a given level of demand, to induce contraction. (Thus even the French—who have been least reluctant to restrain prices—felt constrained to moderate their use of this instrument after the wage

[4] O. Ashenfelter and G. E. Johnson, "Bargaining Theory, Trade Unions, and Industrial Strike Activity," *American Economic Review,* March 1969; John Pencavel, "An Investigation of Industrial Strike Activity in Britain," *Economica,* August 1970.

[5] For a given rate of real wage growth and unemployment rate, incomes policy could also reduce strike activity by lowering the wage increase expected by union members. A study of American strike activity found no statistically significant effect for the period of the *U.S. Guideposts* (see Ashenfelter and Johnson, *op. cit.,* p. 47, fn.9), but there is some evidence that the incidence of strikes in Great Britain was less than predicted during periods of incomes policy under the Labour Government (see Pencavel, *op. cit.,* p. 248).

explosion of 1968, since profits were already depressed.) Although price policies were passed when wage policies proved insufficiently effective or were unavailable, they had to contribute appreciably to wage restraint. In France, they did so. But elsewhere their limited effectiveness reflected this failure to restrain wages. In principle this objective could be accomplished in two ways. It could help to persuade the unions to restrain their wage demands by reassuring their members that other economic interests in the community would not profit from their restraint—that the share of profits would not be increased and that the cost of living would not outpace money wages. This was a major premise on which the British and Danish price policies were erected. Incidentally, it had some appeal to conservative governments (in 1956 in Britain and in 1968 in Denmark) to whom it held out possible hope of winning union hearts by twisting capitalist arms. This approach was reflected in both the British and American formulations of wage-price policy, according to which price reductions were called for in industries with greater-than-average increases in productivity, in order to secure over-all price stability. The desirability of such price reductions was stressed by the British Prices and Incomes Board after the devaluation of 1967 as an essential *quid pro quo* for the unions. The Dutch Minister of Economic Affairs also tried to secure price reductions in 1967.

This type of price restraint would not squeeze profits; it would be consistent with the attainment or maintenance of full employment as well as over-all price stability. But in general the price reductions which are essential to the satisfaction of these two conditions have not been forthcoming. Offered a choice between a reduction in profits via price reduction and a reduction in profits via general deflation, managers of large-scale enterprises might well prefer the latter as the probable lesser of two evils. Thus the outcome of expected loss calculations of businessmen in growth industries seems to have been similar to the conclusions reached by individual unionists.

Price controls might also operate on the employer side of the labor market—by increasing the incentive of management to resist union demands as well as by reducing its incentive and capacity to pay drift. That the Dutch hoped to follow this route (as well as to induce union moderation) is revealed in policies so formulated as generally to prevent increases in labor costs above specified amounts from being reflected in price increases. However, the effectiveness of a policy which has to rely predominantly on restraining employer generosity is bound to be limited, because it imposes on employers the cost—or at least it increases the risk—of taking strikes. And in so doing price policy confronts the government with the disagreeable task of balancing the social utility of industrial peace against the social utility of wage-price stability. (France, where wages were sensitive to price movements and price policies had some effect in restraining wages, looked something like an exception that proved a rule, at least until 1968. But French employers did not have to face strong conventional union pressure.) Thus, the effectiveness of price policy is, like that of mandatory wage restraint, to a critical degree a function of its ability to incline the union side to moderation. But its powers of persuasion have been, for reasons noted above, definitely limited.

LESS OVERFULL EMPLOYMENT?

Given the limitations of incomes policy in coping with the levels of excess demand which have prevailed in Europe, what are the visible alternatives? An obvious alternative would be to throw more of the burden on monetary and fiscal policy and to run the economies at lower levels of employment and capital utilization. Would deflation be any more palatable in the seventies than in the past? If, as has been suggested, price stability has gained ground as a public objective in its own right, has public tolerance of unemployment grown accordingly? Has lack of response to appeals for wage restraint itself implied political tolerance of unemployment on a scale sufficient to yield an acceptable degree of price stability? We have observed that the British followed a more deflationary path towards the end of the sixties, with seeming acceptance of levels of unemployment which were high by postwar standards. These observations suggest, as we have noted, that higher levels of unemployment benefits and related transfer payments might help raise public tolerance of unemployment somewhat, but it might also mean that higher rates of unemployment would then be associated with somewhat less restraint on wage and price movements than otherwise would have been the case.

In short, there is little evidence of a popular will to roost further down on the Phillips curve, or at least far enough down to reconcile the public's employment and price preferences. Is it possible, however, that deflation could be accompanied by policies which could get more mileage in terms of price behavior out of a given (small) reduction in employment and capacity utilization than could have otherwise occurred? That is, is it possible that, if one goes a bit further down the Phillips curve, the possibilities for shifting the curve inward improve? Two leading alternatives are suggested in this connection.

The first is "active labor market policy," which was designed by its Swedish originators to operate in company with moderate fiscal-monetary stringency and to serve as an alternative to incomes policy-cum-excess demand. The object is to minimize structural unemployment and its obverse, "bottleneck" inflation by a battery of policy instruments. The latter include manpower training, relocation subsidies, and improved labor-market information services, on the one hand; and selective demand reflation, designed to channel investment into "depressed" sectors, on the other. Thus, in the absence of over-all excess demand, the task of restraining wages can be entrusted to the natural instincts of the employers, but with a lower cost in terms of unemployment and sacrificed output than would have otherwise been exacted. Of course, active labor-market policy might not shift the Phillips curve sufficiently to preclude some increase in total unemployment. Nevertheless, it could be argued that, by reducing the dispersion of unemployment, active labor-market policy might make a higher average level of unemployment less socially objectionable.

However, evidence on the effectiveness of the Swedish labor-market policies has been conflicting. The policies tend in some respects to increase inflationary pressures, while reducing them in other ways. Moreover, although these policies may well succeed in spreading the burden of unemployment more equally throughout the labor force, this need not have the effect of making a given level of unemployment more palatable politically. The effect of reducing the dispersion of unemployment on the political acceptability of the over-all mean level would be influenced by (a) the relative size (in terms of voting strength) of the high-unemployment and the low-unemployment sectors and (b) the absolute level of unemployment in the low-unemployment sectors. Thus, if the large unemployment sectors form a small proportion of the total electorate or if the initial levels of unemployment in the low-unemployment sectors are extremely low, then the above conclusion might well hold. If, on the other hand, the low-unemployment sectors comprise a strong majority of the electorate or if the low end of the distribution should be characterized by a level of unemployment which is not much below the threshold of political acceptability, the effect of a reduction in the dispersion of unemployment could be a general insistence upon a lower rather than a higher over-all unemployment rate. And if that is not matched by a higher tolerance of inflation, we are back to Square One.

A second way to shift the Phillips curve inward at lower levels of demand might be found through incomes policy itself. Incomes policy might have the effect of inducing employers to exploit their increased bargaining power more fully under these conditions. Such extra resistance, however, would presumably result in more industrial conflict than could otherwise be expected at prevailing levels of slack and unemployment—unless unionists themselves should be more responsive to appeals for wage restraint at somewhat higher levels of unemployment. To the extent that wage drift is reduced, union leaders could "afford" to exercise more restraint under conditions which one of them, in private conversation, carefully characterized as "less overfull employment." On the other hand, at higher levels of unemployment, a published wage norm could act perversely on some unions, as British and Danish experience seems to suggest. The general desire to "beat" the norm in order to justify one's reason for being should not be keener in the absence of excess demand. However, leaders of unions in weak bargaining positions who, in the absence of incomes policy, would find it politically possible to negotiate below-average settlements might find it politically necessary to hold out for guideline increases. (This argument could rationalize British evidence of the apparent effectiveness of norms at unemployment rates below 1.8 per cent but of their ineffectiveness at higher rates.)

Institutional Reform?

In view of the limited public tolerance of unemployment, inflation, strikes, and legal compulsion, would not the direct reduction of institutional restraints on the labor markets, by legal measures, be indicated and effective? Incomes policy itself would generate institutional reform if it worked as advertised, by inducing union restraint; and such reforms as we have observed, would probably include increased centralization of authority within the trade-union movement. However, the classic laissez-faire objective would be to reduce union bargaining strength (at given levels of employment and capacity utilization) and to do so by decentralizing and diffusing wage-setting authority on the union side. Actually, since incomes policy in operation can create stress within trade-union institutions, it can serve as an unwitting agent of decentralization rather than as a centralizing force. But a policy can hardly be advocated for the allegedly beneficial consequences of its probable failure; and so the champions of decentralization properly put forward their structural reforms in competition with incomes policy.

However, to many Europeans it must appear that they have too much, rather than too little, decentralization and that (apart from the requirements of formal incomes policy) the problem is to obtain more centralized control over labor costs. Local plant-level organizations seem to have considerable bargaining power—enough to generate "imitative" wage drift and, especially in the United Kingdom, to retard the level of and rate of increase in productivity. (Analogous examples in the United States are furnished by the highly autonomous locals in the construction and printing industries, where bargaining power would be largely unaffected by legal reforms aimed at breaking up the national unions.) It is a fair inference that, in introducing industrial relations along Taft-Hartley lines, the Heath government in the United Kingdom contemplated an accretion of national-union control over the shop stewards.

Moreover, where greater decentralization might conceivably abate pressure on labor costs, it might well have to be enforced in the product market as well as in the labor market, for union monopoly power is sometimes underwritten to a considerable extent by enterprise monopoly or oligopoly. In small economies, the scope for such decentralization might be so limited as to preclude serious consideration of this alternative. But even where feasible, significant reduction of prevailing levels of concentration in both labor and product markets could entail significant redistribution of incomes and assets. And this no less than higher unemployment and governmental wage or price controls translates into political cost to the would-be reformers.

THE COST OF EFFECTIVENESS

In contrast to its alternatives, incomes policy has been regarded as a costless instrument. This is one reason why its popularity, however tarnished, has managed to survive its failures; a benefit-cost ratio can be quite impressive when the cost is zero. Moreover, even an economically ineffective incomes policy can yield a political payoff. It can enable an incumbent administration to appear (and to be) industrious in fighting inflation, to proceed with popular expansionist measures, under cosmetic cover, and to pin the blame for any inflationary wage and price movements on private selfishness. Such a policy can succeed only in buying a few more years of rake's progress, but for politicians, whose rate of time discount is always high, it is catnip.

Economists too are irresistibly drawn to a minimum-cost policy. Yet they of all people should entertain reservations about the availability of free lunch. The low level of social benefits yielded by incomes policies should invite speculation that the social costs and risks may be too low. For if, as experience indicates, private costs and risks are too high to gain acceptance by the trade unions, part of the burden will have to be shifted on to other shoulders and risks will have to be pooled more widely. This is implicit in various proposals for change and reform raised toward the end of the 1960's as well as in some features of established policy in some European countries.

In the first place, rewards for cooperation would have to be made more tangible, and guarantees would have to be given. It has not been sufficient to assure unionists that wage restraint is conducive to price stability and that price stability is conducive to low unemployment and faster growth and that these in turn would make it possible to raise real labor incomes more rapidly. But to be more precise than this, the authorities would have both to run and to underwrite the risk of policy failure. We have seen that, at the end of the sixties, Dutch union leaders wanted to bargain in real terms; they felt that they had to demonstrate to the members that money wage restraint would in fact be rewarded by bigger increases in real wages than they had been able to obtain in the absence of an effective incomes policy. This implied cost-of-living escalation, which is necessary simply to maintain the share of wages in the national income—but which can serve as a powerful inflationary instrument in its own right. Yet the wage norm adopted in the German Federal Republic in 1966 allowed for an expected increase in consumer prices as well as in productivity and, as we have noted, won a United Nations accolade for "a certain advance towards realism." The Danes, who had installed an automatic escalator after World War I, retained it under incomes policy; and, although they modified it in the freeze of 1963 and debated its elimination in 1967, they chose to subsidize any wage increments which it might generate under a partial price freeze in 1970. The French, who have placed more emphasis on price control than any of the other countries, nevertheless increased the responsiveness of their national minimum wage to change in the cost of living while, at the same time, tying it to the growth rate of the economy. The association of wage escalation and price restraint is interesting; it suggests that a wage-restraint policy with a cost-of-living guarantee might have to be accompanied by some authority to restrain prices directly.

Moreover, just as fiscal and monetary authorities must reach certain reciprocal accommodations, so might these and other senior branches of policy-making have to accept certain restrictions in the interests of incomes policy. Thus, if effective wage restraint requires prior price stability, can the government adopt deflationary devices—like the value-added tax—which themselves raise prices? The Dutch unionists thought not; but increased reliance on such alternatives as direct taxation or monetary restraint might mean purchasing more price stability at a greater cost in terms of foregone investment and growth. On the other hand, the government might find it inadvisable to rely freely on its budgetary powers, if this would impose an extra degree of restraint on its own employees. And, of course, the authorities cannot assume the absence of a trade-off between the over-all degree of deflation applied and the effectiveness of incomes policy: they cannot deflate to the degree desired in the absence of an incomes policy and expect the policy to retain its effectiveness. Finally, other lines of policy-making might have to move actively in support of a desired level of incomes policy effectiveness. Thus, according to some union spokesmen, if an incomes policy designed to redistribute labor income by granting exceptionally large wage increases to low-paid groups proves unenforceable, it should be replaced by an incomes policy which provides for no such exceptions but which is accompanied by fiscal measures designed explicitly to redistribute total income in favor of the poor.

The institutional sensibilities of the unions must also be taken into account if union support is required—that is, if union officers can be expected to respond to external social pressure. The community might respond in two ways to the complaint that incomes policy threatens to deprive the unions of their vital bargaining function. In the first place, it might minimize some adverse consequences of constrained bargaining. It might encourage employer resistance and thus make a wage norm less objectionable because it is more difficult to achieve. The social cost of this alternative would be measured in terms of increased industrial unrest. Or it might find it necessary to provide some legal sanctions, thus affording the cooperative union leader protection against invidious comparisons with potential "rogue elephants" and at the same time providing him with an official whipping boy.

The community might also seek to provide its labor movement with new outlets for its institutional energies. These might be located, figuratively speaking, either above or below the level of wage bargaining. In the former category, one might include involvement of top union leadership in the formulation of social policies which would be designed as alternative ways to achieve some of the goals of traditional collective bargaining. This could involve the corporate approach of *concertation,* with a much expanded agenda, or global bargaining over wage norms, or, more prosaically, increased emphasis on the lobbying and other political activities of the central federation. Another outlet might be provided by affording union officials room at the top of corporate enterprise. This approach was pioneered by the Germans and more recently followed by the Dutch. But such high-level activities which would point to more centralization of power within the national labor movement, would afford more gratification to the paid professionals than to the increasingly restive dues-paying membership. They would be no substitute for measures taken at the level of the grass roots—which point to decentralization.

In the latter context we have referred to "participation," that Gaullist innovation designed to give wage earners a share in decision-making in the workplace or even at the company-wide level. Its popularity has spread in the wake of the worker malaise which it is designed to alleviate. Yet its consequences are uncertain. It could strengthen the continental trade-union movements—or it could give rise to a latter-day version of company unionism. It could pay off in higher productivity—or it could, by denying management the freedom to make changes in advance of employee objection, reduce the rate of growth in productivity. Productivity-bargaining, the British hybrid, which seeks to combine features of both *participation* and wage-bargaining, might point the way to constructive institutional change, especially in countries where the bargaining authority of national industrial unions is already weak. The danger that high wage increases won under productivity-bargaining might ripple out to other groups suggests that its effectiveness presupposes the existence of an effective incomes policy —but it could make an appreciable contribution to such over-all effectiveness.

Thus we believe that, if incomes policy is to play an effective role in reconciling politically acceptable levels of employment with politically acceptable levels of price stability, its scope must be considerably broadened and, in the process, social costs and risks must be accepted. There is no reason to believe that a reasonably efficient policy must contain all cost items discussed in the preceding paragraphs. It appears to us that the most promising—or, perhaps, the least unrealistic—of the innovative alternatives discussed in this concluding section is the guaranteed increase in real wage incomes. We have observed that, in the past, devices to enforce incomes policies were limited in their application by official reluctance to tolerate the levels of industrial unrest required for effective enforcement. Now if incomes policies have operated by holding back real wages—if, that is, they were more effective in restraining money wages than prices—the policies themselves might have tended to increase industrial unrest, which seems to vary inversely with movements in real wages. This would leave the authorities with no effective alternative to deflation. Suppose, on the other hand, that incomes policy were to guarantee an increase in real wage incomes while restraining money wage incomes. Such indexation would magnify the inflationary consequences of policy failure, and it would also restrict the range of fail-safe deflationary instruments available to the authorities, as noted above. On the other hand, the assurance that their incomes would increase more rapidly under a policy of restraint than they had under an inflationary free-for-all would presumably enhance compliance and thus reduce the probable need for deflationary alternatives. By minimizing an important cause of industrial unrest, this policy would likewise reduce reliance on legal instruments of enforcement, while, at the same time increasing their effectiveness as a deterrent to potential rogue elephants. To union leaders it might prove a superior alternative to worker participation, with its uncertain effect on institutional cohesiveness, on the one hand, and productivity on the other. Finally, to the extent that it reduces recourse to deflation and industrial stoppage, such an incomes policy helps to generate the growth in productivity out of which its guarantee can be made good.

But this approach would be only a departure. Important questions of income distribution—how much for investment and growth and how much for the low-paid—would remain, although *concertation* in one form or another would be facilitated. Other groups—property owners and the recipients of transfer incomes—will also require escalator protection against inflation. With all major income categories thus protected, it might prove feasible to set a gearage ratio which would result in less than one-for-one compensation for some untoward rise in prices. But the margin for error in demand management would be narrow; and standby authority over both wages and prices might be required for protection against errors and accidents as well as rogue elephants.

It may be the public judgment that such a policy's risks and costs outweigh its probable benefits. If so, the obvious alternative is acceptance of stop-go, although perhaps with the periodic spells of deflation associated with and possibly softened by short-term policies of wage-price restraint. This is not an heroic solution, nor would it be without social cost. But if unpretentious interventions could minimize "inflationary depression" (the phenomenon referred to at the beginning of this chapter), they could, paradoxically, counter perverse reactions of modern society and help it to approximate a bit more closely the frictionless model of theory which has nourished the goal of noninflationary full employment.